TRASH BAG TALES

& Other Stories from an Accidentally Happy Life

CHARELL STAR

ISBN: 979-8-9919228-0-7

Library of Congress Control Number: 2024926005

A Letter to My Readers:

Welcome to my rollercoaster of a life—a journey marked by positivity, resilience, and a sprinkle of mischief.

Consider this memoir your backstage pass, complete with laughter, tears, and a few moments that will make you question whether I've been living in a dramedy. But hey, who needs fiction when reality is this entertaining?

My story begins in a place that's not often talked about beyond the usual "tragic orphan" tropes. People don't want to think too hard about kids who've been in foster care, and I get it. When you've lived in the system, you see firsthand how rotten the apple has become. Happy endings are rare and sometimes feel a bit accidental. Or, at the very least, you learn early on that if anyone's going to rescue you, it'll have to be yourself. What does that look like? If you're a woman of color who grew up in poverty, it means going into the game with three strikes against you. And that's on a good day!

I guess that's the worst part. But here's the best part: If you can move past your past, you'll have learned a ton. The strongest steel is formed in the hottest fire, as the saying goes. If I can help you skip the part that burns, then this book will have done its job. I wrote it for anyone who needs to see a way forward.

Before you dive in, let me share two things up front. Firstly, like everyone else, my life has progressed in a linear fashion. This narrative, less so. I'm deliberately bumping around by theme, rather than just giving you a birth-to-adulthood account of my life thus far. For me, that feels like a more honest picture of who I am and offers the clearest way for me to share what I've learned.

Secondly, yes, these stories are as true as the sky is blue, but to protect the not-so-innocent (and to avoid any potential lawsuits), I've sprinkled a little fairy dust and changed some names.

Now, don't let the drama fool you; this memoir isn't just a collection of anecdotes. It's a testament to the belief that you can get through life's chaos to the other side with a smile, and that kindness doesn't have to come laced with toxicity.

I've carved out a reputation for being the eternal optimist, the one who insists on seeing the silver lining in even the stormiest clouds. But I'm not about that toxic positivity life. Nope, not here. I firmly believe you can be positive and kind without drowning in saccharine platitudes.

I'm here to share the highs, lows, and everything in between. Why? Because life is messy, complicated, and downright absurd at times. I've bared my soul in these pages, in the hopes that my stories will be a roadmap for those seeking their own voice and power. Life's too short for silent struggles and untold tales.

So, buckle up, my friends. May my misadventures encourage you to embrace your own stories, challenges, and experiences. Let them empower you to be the best version of yourself and remind you never to hide from your past. You never know the impact your authenticity may have on others or the change it can inspire in the world.

Here's to positivity without the poison, and to kindness that feels like a warm hug rather than a forced action. Let the adventure begin!

Contents

For everyone learning how to heal and grow. Keep going.

PROLOGUE
Eat Cake for Breakfast

On the morning of my 30th birthday, I, Charell Star, whose default happy place is snuggled in my bed, woke up early and excited. Walking through my recently roommate-free apartment towards the shower, I could not stop radiantly smiling. This was my first adult birthday that no longer required me to have a roommate to afford my condo's mortgage. In fact, it was the first time in my life since I was thrown into foster care that I didn't have to live with a roommate at all. I cranked up my music–a little India Arie and Beyoncé–and hopped in the shower.

I did my makeup, put on some warm but cute clothes—it was February in New York City, after all—and headed towards the door. *Carmen*, an Italian opera I'd always wanted to see, was playing at the Metropolitan Opera House. I'd seen a movie version of it when I was a kid and fell in love with the music. As a child, I knew to never ask for tickets to an opera, no matter how much I loved it. For one, show tickets were a luxury none of my foster or bio families could afford. Besides that, I would have been made fun of for even admitting I liked opera. There's only so many times a kid from Harlem can endure being called "bougie" before you decide that keeping quiet is just easier.

But that was then. Today, I was an adult who lived in a judgment- and now people-free home, and the show I wanted to see was offering discounted $20 seats if you were in the line early enough to snag them.

My plan was to leave my condo in Queens, grab breakfast, hop on the subway to Manhattan, and be in line by 9 a.m.—three hours before the box office opened. I had plenty of time. It was only 7 a.m., and the train ride to Manhattan was only 20 minutes on the express train. *It's going to be an amazing day*, I thought to myself as I went to leave my condo.

But, as I pulled at the knob to open the door, I felt the doorknob come loose and remain in the palm of my hand. I looked down at my hand to confirm that the doorknob was indeed no longer attached to the white metal door but instead in my gloved palm. Instinctively, I tried to place the knob back on the door to get it to open, but it wouldn't turn the cylinder. I stood there laughing in disbelief. I was actually locked in my apartment on my birthday!

I remained next to the door—in case I heard someone walk by and I could call for help—and thought through my options for escape. I knew just about everyone on the building floor, and they all left early every morning for work or to drop their kids off at school. Buzzing my neighbors wouldn't help. I could call one of my friends to come help me get out. Once they were there, I could slip the key under the door, and they could let me out. But it was a weekday, and all my friends would be at work by now. Even if one of them could come and release me, it would take hours for them to arrive, and I'd still be stuck with a broken door.

I could call the condo's maintenance company for help, but I knew from past experiences that they would take longer than tunneling through the wall, Shawshank Redemption-style. Since I didn't want to be locked in my apartment all day, I did the only thing that made sense. I unzipped my coat, removed my gloves and earmuffs, and put them away in the closet. Then, I turned, walked into the kitchen, opened the fridge, grabbed the bottle of "emergency celebration" champagne that I always keep handy, and popped it open.

I secured a pretty purple champagne flute from the CD storage unit that I'd DIYed into a pantry/glassware holder and topped it off with bubbly. I grabbed my leftovers from dinner the night before out of the fridge and whisked them into the microwave. When it beeped, I transferred the cheeseburger, fries, and half-slice of cake—along with my glass of champagne—to my kitchen bar counter. I sat in my stool, raised my glass of effervescence, and toasted myself.

About halfway through my makeshift breakfast of burger and bubbles, I whipped out my phone and searched for emergency locksmiths on Google. By the time the locksmith arrived nearly three hours later, my champagne bottle was just about empty, my cake was long gone, and I was all smiles. I'd watched (actually, re-watched) *Ever After,* my absolute favorite Cinderella movie—which only beats out the Whitney Houston-and-Brandy version by a hair because the *Ever After* heroine's obsession with reading rivals my own—and spent much of the morning responding to cute birthday texts from my friends.

After 90 minutes–and $300—the locksmith was able to break me out of my condo and replace the door lock. By that time, I knew it was too late for me to get the discount show tickets. They usually got snapped up quickly, which is why I had planned to wait in line so early in the first place. I shrugged off the morning mishap as a sign from the universe that I wasn't supposed to see *Carmen* just yet and called my friend Heather to see if she wanted to do a last-minute dinner with me to celebrate my birthday. She was in; so, I headed to the city to b-day shop and met her after work at an inexpensive but shockingly fancy Chinese restaurant we both liked near her office. We ate, drank, and laughed for hours.

It was one of the most unforgettable and absolute best birthdays I've ever had. Since then, I've started all my annual birthday celebrations the same way: by popping a bottle of Veuve Clicquot, my favorite champagne, and having a slice of (or sometimes an entire) chocolate cake. I enjoy both throughout the day until I've had my fill.

This small ritual reminds me that I get to set the tone for my own happiness on my birthday… and on every other day in my life. The unexpected will happen, parts of life will just suck, but how I deal with it matters. I stopped being a victim of my circumstances a long time ago, and I'm just not willing to compromise anymore. I have the power to shape my own happiness, navigate challenges, and find joy in the midst of life's unpredictability. I get to decide the energy I bring to every situation and how much of it I will extend to life's curveballs.

I did eventually make it to *Carmen*, by the way. It took a little longer, but this time I didn't have to wait in line in the cold for discount tickets. So, consider this my invitation to put the book down for a moment. Grab your favorite beverage (alcoholic or otherwise) and your favorite treat. I'm waiting here to toast to you.

PART I
Surviving & Growing

CHAPTER 1
Follow the Recipe

My memory goes back so far that people often find it hard to believe that I can recall events from my early childhood. It's not that I remember everything, but there are a number of moments that live in my head quite clearly from years before memories are conventionally thought to form.

I distinctly remember an incident when I was still in diapers, playing with my little cousins. A fireman loudly banged on the door, urging us to open up because there was a fire in our building. One of the older kids, just tall enough to reach the door lock, let him in. The fireman in his heavy, dark-colored coat and thick boots instructed our small group not to leave the apartment and to avoid the hallway. With that, he closed the door, and we resumed our unsupervised play in the tiny, adult-less space.

Another vivid memory involves an accidental burn from my mom's cigarette during an outing when I was too young to be in school with the older kids. I think she had me for a day visit. While chatting with her friends, she unintentionally brushed her lit cigarette against my forehead as I approached. I still recall the stinging pain and the look of surprise on her face. Despite the sudden pain, her tight embrace and tearful apology made me feel safe and loved. I knew I wasn't allowed to live with my mom. I remember the low voices whispering that she needed to "get clean" and the loud reminders for her to have me back "on time." As she held me close, I remember hoping she wouldn't get yelled at when she got me home.

I can also recall trips to the bodega across the street from the apartment I lived in with my great-grandma (my GG) for the first few years of my life. We would drop in whenever we were heading downtown to her doctor's office, most likely to escape the heat or cold as we waited for the bus to appear, depending on the time of year. Before I could count money, she'd lift me high enough to dump my child-size purse, filled with quarters, on the bodega counter to pay for my red Icee that she'd let me buy every time we stopped in. The store owner chuckled as he took a couple of coins, dropping them into his register. He gathered the rest and placed them back in my purse along with a white napkin to prevent my hands from staining.

I may not have known how to count money, but I'm quite sure the first digit I recognized was the number three. From a neighbor's apartment, I'd watch number three subway trains entering and leaving the 148th Street station for hours on end. The subway tunnel for that line began and ended there, and with a pair of binoculars and a wooden chair conveniently stationed by the window, I always had the perfect vantage point. This is also the first subway I remember riding. Too small to pay, I would sneak under the turnstile to enter the station. Descending a giant flight of stairs to the platform, I'd eagerly board the waiting train, find a seat near a window, and climb up and sit on my knees to peer outside once the journey began. As it was the first and last stop on the line, there was never a need to wait for a train; one was always there, doors open, welcoming us aboard.

Many of my oldest and best memories are from the time I lived with my great-grandmother in her high-rise apartment, a few steps away from where the number three train begins and ends. I remember grocery shopping with her in the market right on our block, during which she would give me a quarter to ride the small mechanical horse right outside the store once we were done. I recall her buying coconut cakes from the freezer section and letting me have a slice when we were back in the apartment. I didn't like the furry flakes of coconut, so I'd only eat the layers of cake beneath the icing. Sometimes, she would buy a chocolate cake from the freezer section instead of the coconut one, and I'd gobble up both the icing and cake. I'm fairly sure that's where my lifelong love for chocolate cake began.

I also recall helping her push her shopping cart back and forth to the market. It had four wheels: two big ones in the back and two small ones in the front. It folded up, and she'd walk while pulling the flat frame behind her. Sometimes, she'd keep it open fully and place me inside of it. I'd sit on the black wire frame as she pushed me along the way. I remember the route we would take on our shopping walks. We'd walk along the building grounds, passing kids on the playground with the giant concrete turtles, and slowly climb the mountain of stairs that would leave my great-grandmother out of breath.

We'd take the longer way back to the apartment that avoided the stairs and allowed us to walk down the ramp sandwiched between the other side of the playground and the complex's outdoor pool.

My great-grandmother and I would take the elevator back up to her apartment, and I spent most of my days running between the living room and the dining room or engaging in one of my favorite activities—jumping out the window. My GG's bedroom window opened onto the balcony, and I would race into her bedroom, climb onto the ledge of the window, and jump out onto a cushioned outdoor sofa that lived just below her window on the balcony. Then I'd roll off the sofa, run across the balcony threshold that opened to the dining room, through the kitchen, and past the bathroom, and turn right into her bedroom and do it again. Doing this kept me happily entertained for hours.

I vividly remember cooking with my great-grandmother in her galley-style kitchen. We made every meal together, but my fondest memories are of our breakfasts. She would lay out fruits and veggies for me to wash and slice. The sink was on the opposite counter from the stove and the refrigerator. She'd push a chair from the adjoining dining room up to the end of the counter, and I'd pull myself up onto the dining chair. From there, I would climb onto the yellowing, peeling countertop and walk on the counter to the sink in the center. Sitting with my legs in the sink, I'd turn on the water, individually pick up the apples, carrots, celery, oranges, or other combinations of produce, and run them one by one under the water, rubbing away the grit as she'd taught me. After each one was clean, I'd place it in the large white colander that lived on the counter. Once finished, I'd let her know and then let myself off the counter by reversing my steps.

My great-grandmother would move the full colander to the opposite counter near the stove and slide the chair to the counter on that side. I'd climb on it and, standing fully, begin to cut up the fruits and veggies with a butter knife she'd leave on the counter for me. I'd make big wedge cuts, using the full force of my upper body to press through each item. Carrots were always the hardest to cut. The knife wouldn't quite go through, so I learned to push the dull blade as far in as I could and then pull it out, turn the carrot to the other side, and try to make a second cut so that it would meet the first in the middle. Once I had finished cutting everything, she'd pull a few apple slices from the batch and place them on a plate for me.

The rest of the roughly sliced items were destined for the big metal juicer that lived on the countertop next to the stove. She'd take care of using the very loud juicer, and then we'd move on to my favorite part: making eggs. My GG would place three eggs that she retrieved from the fridge in a small bowl in front of me on the counter. I carefully cracked each egg on the side of a large bowl right next to it and let the yolks drop down into the bowl. Sometimes, a piece of shell would fall into the bowl, and I'd have to fish it out using a larger piece of eggshell.

Next, she'd have me pour some salt from a cylindrical container into my hand, and I'd use my index finger and thumb to pinch the smallest amount and sprinkle it softly into the bowl. We'd also add some black pepper and onion powder that I would lightly shake directly into the bowl. My grandmother would hand me a teacup-sized glass of milk, which I would pour into the eggs. She'd fish her old-school hand mixer from the drawer and hand it to me. I'd place it in the bowl while she held onto the lip of the bowl and manually turned the metal crank on the mixer, making the two beaters at the bottom spin and combine the eggs, milk, and spices.

Once everything was combined, she'd place a frying pan on the stovetop and turn it on. The burner would make a faint clicking sound before the fire would jump out and curve underneath the pan. From a stick of butter sitting on the counter, I'd deftly slice a sliver with my unsharpened knife and lean over—still standing on my chair—and place it into the pan. I'd watch while it melted and guide the thick stick around with my knife to make sure it coated every part of the circular pan. As I finished, my GG would gently pour the liquid mixture into the pan.

I'd be leaning over the pan, waiting for it to start changing from the slightly slimy liquid into a solid. As it transformed, I'd use a metal spatula to push the newly formed solid portion of eggs up so the liquid would rush beneath it. I'd do this until there was no more liquid in the frying pan, and the eggs had taken on the circular shape of the pan. My GG would then hand me a slice of cheese she had removed from the plastic wrapper, and I'd place it in the center of the eggs. She'd hold my hand as we'd flip one edge of the eggs onto the other, folding it in half.

As the eggs finished cooking, she'd have me start making our morning toast. Sometimes I could do the entire process by myself. I'd pick up the large loaf of sliced white bread and hug the plastic-wrapped bag with both arms close to my chest. Once I had it secured, I'd use one hand to slide off the plastic tie that kept it closed and pull out two slices of bread, resting them on a plate she'd left on the counter for me. Then I'd attempt to reattach the plastic tie to seal the bread. Most days, I couldn't get it back on the bag and would simply hold the bagged loaf up in my arms, and my great-grandma would reattach it for me. Some days it was hard for her to do too—she'd rub the palm of her hands, so I knew it was difficult for her. On those days, she'd toss the plastic tie in the open-lidded trashcan that lived in the corner of the dining room that met the kitchen and tie the end of the bread bag in a knot to close it.

I'd pop the two slices of bread into the metal toaster, push the lever down, and wait for it to pop back up moments later. After that, my GG would plate everything and move it all to the dining table for us to enjoy. During breakfast, we'd eat and chat about anything and everything. Mainly, I'd rattle off a bunch of questions to her that had been running through my mind, like "Why are quarters round?" or "Do buses sleep at night?" or "Can I have M&M's today?"

She'd typically smile and indulge me with answers to those types of questions. But some questions were harder than others to answer. I'd ask, “Is my mom going to sleep over?” or “Is my dad going to pick me up today?” Those received a different response. She’d sometimes frown and say, “We’ll see,” or simply tell me to take another bite of my food. Our daily ritual of making breakfast was so routine I can’t think of a single day we didn’t do it together while I lived with her. The closest we ever veered from the custom was one day when she turned her back to me while I was making our eggs.

On this day, for some unknown reason, a random thought popped into my head: If a pinch of salt made the eggs taste good, a lot of salt would make them even better! So, instead of pouring some salt into my hand and adding a pinch to the liquid mixture—as I did every other day—I tilted the cylindrical container of salt and let the pretty crystals rain down into the bowl. I followed all our other standard preparation steps and said nothing to my GG about my recipe tweak.

When we sat down for breakfast, I had a big smile on my face and patiently waited for my GG to take a bite of her eggs. When she finally did, she looked right at me and smiled—well, more like half-smiled. She seemed to be biting her lips as well. I was certain that she loved it and I had done a great job with my little addition.

GG got up from the table and headed to the kitchen. She came back to the spot where the dining room met the kitchen and stood there for a moment. As I lifted my fork to take a bite of the eggs on my plate, I saw something fall from her mouth into the trash from the corner of my eye. I didn’t have too much time to think about what she was doing since a salt bomb exploded in my mouth the second that eggy fork hit my tongue. I spit my bite back onto my plate and looked at my GG, feeling disgusted and defeated for the first time in my young life. She gave me a real smile, sat back down at the table, and simply told me to eat my toast and apple slices. She didn’t mention the eggs once as we ate around them and continued our breakfast in our regular fashion—with my endless questions and her smiling answers.

The next morning, we resumed our breakfast preparation as always. My GG made no mention of the error I made the day before. She didn’t need to. And her welcoming me right back to the kitchen was all the encouragement I needed to reflect, regroup, and try again. And, when it came time to spice the eggs mixture, I intently added only a *single* pinch of salt.

As I look back, this egg debacle is one of my favorite childhood memories. It has shaped me in so many ways, fortifying my love for cooking and securing my belief that salt should be used sparingly, and cementing my other belief that true care shows itself not in applause for our victories, but in the grace it offers our mistakes.

Over the years, there's been so much big and small that I've gotten wrong—sometimes because I thought I knew better and sometimes because I just didn't. In these moments, I use what my GG taught me and give myself time to reflect on my mistake and then try to get it right, to do it better the next go-round. Since then, I've sought out friends and mentors who follow this same model. Do they give me space to make things right—offering support, kindness, or the gift of grace? Those are the people who I welcome back to my own table time and again. It's the people around us who feed our hearts.

CHAPTER 2
Keep Your Courage

I DIDN'T GET TO have breakfast on the day the social worker came and took me from my great-grandmother's. I woke up to find a large black trash bag taller than me by the door, filled with a bunch of my things. I didn't think to ask what it was for or why it was there, because not long after I had walked into our living room, a woman—a social worker—had scooped me in her arms, grabbed the bag, and taken me out of the only home I had ever known. She dropped me off in what I believe was my first foster home.

My foster parents were very cruel and abusive, and I lived in fear of being beaten or yelled at just about every moment of the day. The only other kid in the house was their older, biological daughter. She was at least 10 years older than me, and her favorite pastime was coming up with new ways to be mean to me and make me cry. It didn't take much to get me to cry then—or even now if I'm being honest. I'm just a sensitive person. She'd say the meanest things to me about the way I looked or smelled, how my hair was nappy, or my teeth were crooked, and then she'd just smile and laugh as I cried. I'd usually try not to cry too loud because I didn't want to get hit by her parents for making too much noise.

This went on for months, until I was moved without warning. I came downstairs to find a black trash bag at the door and was whisked off to another foster home. I was there for a while before another trash bag appeared, and I was suddenly moved to another home that barely registers in my memory. In all, I was in the first three homes for about two to three years. The exact amount of time is hard to say, partly because I was so young and just tried to stay out of everyone's way to avoid being hurt, and partly because before I really even got adjusted to the third home, a social worker was already holding a black trash bag in the doorway.

Instead of taking me to a stranger's home, this time the social worker took me to live with my father and my father's girlfriend in what is known as a "kinship" placement. I was still in foster care but was placed with "relatives" while my permanent living arrangements were still being determined by the courts. I'm not certain if they were engaged or married at the time, but my father was out of jail and so my social worker must have deemed it a safe place to live.

His girlfriend had three children of her own, two from a previous relationship as well as my brother who she had with my father. As foster placements go, it wasn't the worst home I'd been dropped into. She tended to be quick with the belt when we kids did anything wrong, but I did my best to stay out of the way and ended up having some really enjoyable experiences there. I got to attend school regularly, she let us go to the park to play, and she even taught me how to ride a bike.

It was the first time—and only time—I lived with my father, but I only have two clear memories of him during this period. One was of him eating. There was a really large bowl in the house, the size you would use to mix a cake in or leave dough in to rise. That particular bowl was his cereal bowl. He'd pour an *entire* box of cereal into the bowl and eat all of it in one sitting. I remember thinking *that's a lot of cereal* and wondering how big your stomach must have to be to eat that much at once. It made for a pretty funny scene because it was never breakfast time when he'd be eating, and he'd be sitting in the oddest places. I'd get home from school, and he'd be munching on his bowl of cereal at like 3:30 in the afternoon on a stool in the living room or sitting on his bed. Although I thought it was a funny sight, I knew better than to laugh or ask why he did this. There was no need to risk the belt.

The other memory of my father is sadder. I'd been living with him and his girlfriend for a while—at least a few months—when us kids got home from school, and he just wasn't there. I don't remember anyone specifically telling me that he'd gone back to jail. Maybe I overheard his girlfriend talking on the phone about it, but somehow, I automatically knew when he wasn't there.

One day, his girlfriend took us to see him in court. I don't remember if she took all four of us kids, but I remember my brother and I were there. Since we were pretty young, we ended up not being allowed into the actual courtroom and waited in the hallway alone. At some point, my brother and I were standing near the door to the courtroom when it swung open, and we saw our father. I don't remember his face, but it was the first time I saw anyone in handcuffs. And not just handcuffs; there were cuffs on his ankles too, with a chain that connected to the ones on his hands. I don't think he even saw us; the door opened and closed so fast. The face I do remember was my brother's as he started to cry.

An interesting fact about my brother and me is that we're only two months apart. There's a lot to unpack there: my father's relationship with my mom, his relationship with his girlfriend/wife, her relationship with me, and of course, my relationship with my brother. As an adult, I've thought a lot about the complicated emotions that this very messy situation created, but as a child, I didn't even know to think about it at all. I knew my brother was slightly older than me and I think a grade ahead of me because of when his birthday landed, but he was a kid, and he was kind, and I was just happy he was there with me. To be honest, it helped that I also never felt like he was more advanced than me. In fact, my grades were usually better than his on our tests and report cards. I was always quick to grab a book where he preferred to play a video game. And he despised watching *Sesame Street* where I would beg the older kids to give me my TV turn so I could watch it.

In the entire time I lived with him, I never thought of him as smarter than me, but in that instance, he proved he was as we caught that glimpse of our father in the courtroom. While my brain was stuck on how small the handcuffs looked, wondering how hard it would be to walk with cuffs on your ankles, his brain had fully processed the truth of the matter:

Our father wasn't coming home.

In the weeks that passed after that court date, no one told us what he'd done. They only said he wouldn't be home for a long time. There was no explanation on how long "a long time" was or talk of our feelings on the matter. It was just a fact that we needed to accept and so I stopped asking questions about it. I also knew not to ask the obvious question—*what happens to me now?*—since I knew no one would answer that for me either.

I didn't have to wonder about my living status for too long. Soon after my father went away, my social worker started bringing me for visits with my grandmother on my mother's side. My grandmother is not to be confused with my great-grandmother (my GG) who I lived with before I entered foster care. This was my mom's mother, and I'd never known her before the social worker started taking me to visits with her. To be fair, I'm sure she met me when I was a baby, but I have no memories of her before the visits began.

Our time together was always uncomfortable for me. She acted nice, but my gut told me she really wasn't. Maybe it was the years in care, of being treated as nothing more than an obligation, or perhaps it was the fact that I was still quite young and could recognize pretend play when I saw it. During our outings, she would usually take me to a diner or restaurant and ask me a ton of questions about my father's girlfriend: *How many people lived in the apartment? What did they do all day? What did we eat? Where did we go? Do I know where she worked? Did other men come by? Did I miss any school? Did I like living there?*

Each time we met, she'd ask me a lengthy list of questions—some she'd asked before and some that were new. I didn't know why she wanted to know so much about my father's girlfriend and her family, but I didn't want to make her angry by not answering her questions, so I did. This went on for several visits. The social worker would pick me up and drop me off to meet with my grandmother. She'd take me someplace to eat for lunch and pepper me with questions. Then the social worker would pick me up and take me back home to my father's girlfriend's apartment. I was young and didn't think too much about what was going on, but I do wish I had. I might not have been so gullible when she threw a curve ball at me.

During one outing, instead of taking me to lunch she took me to run an errand. I don't remember what the "errand" was, but I remember she told me to stay outside a store while she went inside. I don't know how long I was standing there but I remember it felt like forever. People were staring at me as they walked past. It must have been a really odd sight: this little kid standing alone outside a store on a busy street in New York City looking a thousand percent out of place. I stood there so long, my legs got tired, and I wanted to sit down so badly, but I knew sitting on the dirty ground would get me in trouble, so I just kept shifting my weight between my legs. I was also really hungry because I hadn't eaten anything since breakfast, and it was pretty late in the afternoon. When she finally came back out, she asked me if I wanted to go to McDonald's. Now, as a kid, there was nothing I wanted to eat more than a McDonald's Happy Meal. Not only did I get a burger and fries, but it came with a toy, and I could use the box the food came in as a house for my dolls.

But as quickly as she made the offer, she said that, actually, we didn't have time to go since we would go over our visitation time, and she had to get me back to the social worker. I really wanted to go to McDonald's. So, I told her that my father's girlfriend wasn't home yet and probably wouldn't care if I was late. My father's girlfriend had told all us kids that she'd be home late before she had left for work that morning, and she had never made any comments to me about spending time with my grandmother. I didn't think she'd mind her keeping me out a little later at all. My grandmother smiled and took me to McDonald's.

After she got our food, she left me at the table while I was eating and went outside for a while. I didn't mind her leaving me alone too much this time because I was sitting down and finally eating. She came back in before I finished my meal and then let me go play in the McDonald's playpen. It was the first time she'd ever let me do that, and I had a ball playing with the random other kids there. It felt like we were there for hours, and we must have been because it was dark when she finally said we needed to go meet the social worker. I could tell that my father's girlfriend was mad when the social worker dropped me off.

As soon as I was inside the apartment, she sent me straight to my room and told me to stay there.

I honestly didn't know why, since she had never shown much interest in my visits with my grandmother except to ask me, "Did you have a good time?" whenever I returned home. From my room that I shared with my brother in the very back of the apartment, I could hear her on the phone talking to someone. She was really angry, and her voice carried through the halls. I couldn't make out everything, but I was able to piece together that a foster care social worker showed up to inspect the apartment because *I told* my grandmother that "there were no adults at home with the kids."

I overheard her say on the phone, "I'm not gonna fight for custody for a liar and have these people coming to my home." That wasn't what I had told my grandmother at all, but I never got the chance to tell her my side of what actually transpired that day. I can't remember when I was moved out of the home, that same day or a few days later, but it happened very soon after.

The move was a blur, but I remember my social worker saying to me, "You must have really wanted to live with your grandmother and knew just how to make it happen." That statement stung because it just wasn't true. I didn't want to live with my grandmother. I didn't even think she really liked me, but no one had ever asked me. I wasn't certain that I would have wanted to remain living with my father's girlfriend, but at least my brother lived there too. And no one had told me that they were *fighting* for custody of me. And, worst of all, I never told my grandmother that there were no adults at home with the kids and wouldn't have said anything at all if I knew she was going to try to get my father's girlfriend in trouble.

I didn't voice any of this to the social worker, though, because I felt guilty that she'd already branded me a liar and I didn't think the truth mattered now anyway. At some point, she dropped me off to live with my grandmother. I don't remember if I got to say goodbye to my brother or pack my things. I just remember entering the darkly lit wooden vestibule of my grandmother's apartment building and riding the small, darkly lit elevator up to her place. As it turned out, this darkness hinted toward some of the trouble to come.

When you entered the apartment there was a really tiny box-style kitchen to the left where she'd placed a small rectangular table with two chairs against the wall. This is where I would come to eat most of my meals while I lived with her. Immediately past the kitchen was the living room, which she kept immaculate. There was a sofa that I was rarely allowed to sit on and a large wooden box that housed a huge TV that would rise out of it when a button was pressed on a remote. There was also a tiny, child-sized grey chair made of foam that unfolded into a bed, which is where I slept. I was used to sleeping on the floor in different foster homes, so sleeping on the thin foam mattress wasn't so bad. The only annoying part was that she made me strip the mattress and fold it back into a chair and put away the sheets every morning because she didn't like having a "bed" in the living room. I would then have to unfold the mattress and sheet and make the bed every night before I went to sleep.

Beyond the living room, there was a bathroom that was big enough for a tub and pedestal sink, and just past that was the apartment's only bedroom. Through the door, to the left, there was a giant bed with a cream-colored lacquered headboard and matching nightstands flanking each side. Atop them were matching lacquered lamps, and under the lamp farthest from the door was a crystal ashtray. Across from the bed was a large dresser, not a tall one but a low, long one with a huge matching mirror. On top were various perfume bottles on a mirrored tray with gold trim and really fancy 24-carat gold jewelry. I didn't know what a carat was but would come to understand from overhearing my grandmother's conversations with her friends that 24-carat was hard to come by and therefore the best when it came to jewelry. The bedroom also held a large closet that housed her expansive wardrobe of pantsuits, furs, and leather purses with logos on them. Everything in her room felt rich and pretty but in a way that felt wrong and out of place.

By far the most shocking thing in the room was positioned to the left of the bedroom door. There sat a white crib that housed none other than my baby sister, who was lying down with her eyes open drinking from her bottle. Until the moment I walked in that room, I didn't know I had another sibling, but here she was. She was a long and skinny baby, with very wide eyes and an even wider smile.

From that moment, she became my responsibility. I'd feed her bottles, get her dressed when we went out, put her down for a nap or bed, and change her diapers. Most days, my grandmother would wake me up with a rough shake and I'd get my sister changed and fed and then head out to school early enough to have a free breakfast in the cafeteria. I needed to move quickly because every moment I spent lingering was a moment that could set off my grandmother and I'd be met with a slap to my face or punch to my back for moving slowly. My school was about 10 blocks from the apartment, but to my tiny child legs it felt like it was miles away, especially when it snowed. I'd walk the reverse route at the end of the school day and stay with our next-door neighbor who watched my sister and me until my grandmother got home. Sometimes she'd arrive right after *Jeopardy!* went off, and sometimes we would have already been asleep for hours when we'd be awakened to head back to our apartment.

Some mornings, I'd wake up in the apartment and my grandmother wouldn't be there. She'd never tell me ahead of time that she wouldn't be coming home, so it was always a surprise. Usually, this would happen on a Saturday or Sunday, so I'd get up, change and feed my sister, and pour myself some cereal and entertain her for the day. We weren't allowed to use her TV, so I'd mainly read to her or play silly games to make her laugh. If there was other food in the fridge, I'd make that for lunch or dinner—usually a sandwich—or if the fridge was bare, I'd knock on our next-door neighbor's door and ask for something to eat. Our neighbor was an amazing cook, and she always would make me a plate of whatever she had available. I'd eat it in our apartment and then get back to caring for my sister for the evening or rest of the weekend.

On one occasion, I woke up on a school day and my grandmother wasn't home. I don't remember all the thoughts that went on in my head except that I didn't want to miss school. So, I got dressed, got my sister dressed and fed her, and took her to our neighbor's apartment to watch her. I do remember my neighbor asking me where my grandmother was. I told her I didn't know but that I needed to get to school. She took my sister from my arms, and I went back to our apartment to grab my backpack, let the door slam locked behind me, and headed to the elevator to get on my way. I made it in time for breakfast and had a fairly normal day at school. When I returned, at the end of the school day, I knocked on our apartment door which went unanswered. So, I turned and knocked on my neighbor's door. She let me in to join my sister, and I got started on my homework. Later in the evening she fed us, and we just waited for my grandmother to return.

It was late at night when my grandmother finally knocked on the door. She thanked our neighbor for watching us but didn't ever say where she had been. They talked in hushed tones for a while, and then we were herded next door. When we were back in the apartment, she told me matter-of-factly that it was past my bedtime. So, I changed my sister, placed her in her crib, unfolded my mattress, and went to sleep. The next day my grandmother woke me up, and I headed to school as usual.

If I'm being honest, my grandmother terrified me, and most of my time living with her was awful. She'd wake me up in the middle of the night and, with wild eyes, accuse me of stealing from her. She'd have the contents of my backpack—my schoolbooks and pencils—thrown on the floor and tell me something of hers was missing: money, a necklace, a lighter, or some other random thing. I'd deny taking anything (because I hadn't) and she'd threaten to burn my hands if she ever caught me. I'd go back to bed shaking and on the verge of tears but would always try to hold them back because I knew she'd hit me if I cried. It was super easy to trigger her—although I did my best to try not to—especially if I took too long to find something she'd asked me to fetch or if I stared off in the distance too long. I'd feel a hard punch on the center of my back or a random object hit my body and know she was mad. I can still vividly hear the ring of the bell of the corded phone receiver that hung on the wall outside the kitchen as she slammed it across my face because I was taking too long to eat something she'd made. She was quick to take offense at any perceived slight or insolence and answer it in some violent way. I knew not to cross her, not to question her, and to avoid upsetting her at all costs.

But she didn't punish me for going to school that weekday morning she disappeared, even though I had told our neighbor she left us alone and, I'm certain, incurred an extra non-budgeted babysitting bill she had to pay. And, although my grandmother would disappear with no warning several more times while my sister and I lived with her, she never again did it on a school day.

When I'm feeling generous, I imagine that even she believed that my education was so important that it couldn't be left to chance. But the truth is, I think that I just terrified her that day. After all the beatings, the mental and emotional abuse she dished out, there was still something I loved more than I feared her: my education. And the idea that I would do anything to not lose out on it wasn't worth the risk for her.

When I think back on the years of living with my grandmother, I take comfort in that fact. That even though I was small, scared, and scarred, a part of me was still unflappable, and even unbothered. I didn't even know I had that spark in me, but she could see it and couldn't put it out. There have been more than a few moments in my life where I have felt overwhelmed, like I was failing and couldn't handle what was coming next. And usually after a therapeutic cry—or good glass of wine—I remember that my spirit didn't stay lit on my darkest days to be dimmed now.

CHAPTER 3
Resilience Is a Gift

I've often wondered how a woman in her mid-to-late seventies came to be responsible for a toddler when there were lots of much younger, able-bodied family members around who could have taken me in. I'm guessing at my great-grandmother's (GG's) age, but I believe she was at least that old when I came to live with her, as the lines of her well-lived face rising like the sunrays into a smile are the oldest memory I have implanted into my brain.

Full of boundless energy, I'd run all over her apartment, contorting my tiny body to hide within the doors of her wooden coffee table or inside the cabinet beneath the sink in the bathroom—a joyful chaos inserted into the order she'd spent a lifetime building. It would take her a while, but with a smile she'd locate me, and I never knew how, but I bet the giggles that escaped from behind the closed doors might have been a clue. I don't ever remember her telling me I was wanted or loved; that truth was in her big smiles, in long hugs and warm kisses on my cheeks, and in the leisurely breakfasts we made together. These intangible gifts of belonging were a truth that she implanted so deeply within me that it became core to my entire being.

I held on to this belief during the entire time I was in kinship care and living with my grandmother (not my GG). I knew what it was to be loved and wanted, so my grandmother's version of it always rang false and hollow.

One time, my grandmother beat me incessantly because something she was looking for was missing and she was convinced I'd stolen it, even though I hadn't. The next day, my birthday, I came back from school to find the apartment filled with her adult friends and a pretty blue dress wrapped in a box and bow. She insisted I open it immediately and wear it for the party. Her friends complimented her kindness, cheering her childrearing skills between drinks as I sat stiffly on the couch, terrified to move and get the dress wrinkled or dirty. Throughout the party, she'd sit next to me and instruct me to tell everyone what a "wonderful grandmother" she was, and I'd oblige, saying things like, "You're the best grandmother in the world." She'd walk away smiling, and I just continued to sit there, fake smiling and holding back tears. She hadn't even bothered to invite my babysitters' kids, friends who lived next door, to the party. But it wasn't meant to be a celebration for me.

Not too long after, her "roommate" moved into the one-bedroom apartment and things got better for a while. We called her Titi, and for dinner, she would make my sister and me Spanish rice with octopus and olives in it. She'd guilt our grandmother into letting us watch TV at the kitchen table—something I would have never dared to ask for. Titi was calm and even keeled where my grandmother was wild and irrational. If my grandmother was darkness, Titi was light. On New Year's Eve, she even let me have a small sip of champagne from her glass—starting my lifelong love affair with the bubbly drink that tickled my nose. Things were better with Titi around, and I didn't think anything of it when my sister and I were sent to live with Titi's family in the projects.

It was an apartment already bursting at the seams with four generations within its walls. A Puerto Rican flag hung in the living room that had been converted into a private bedroom for the oldest daughter, her husband (or boyfriend, I'm not sure which), and their little boy. The boy was a baby, younger than my sister, able to walk and in the process of being potty trained. He wasn't particularly good at it and whenever I took him to the bathroom, he'd pee everywhere, and I'd have to clean it up. I was already used to cleaning up after my baby sister, so helping with another baby didn't bother me too much; I just wished he wouldn't pee on the floor so much. Their mother, grandmother, and young daughter a few years older than me lived in the apartment as well.

Their grandmother was much older than mine and reminded me of my GG, with well-lived skin and endless patience. I'd race into the kitchen and find her sitting at her perch, a padded chair at the head of the small kitchen table; her face would light up and she'd start talking to me. The words coming in rapid succession, inflections, and intonations were all I was able to assess. I spoke not a word of Spanish and she didn't speak any English, but I liked that she talked to me, and she was my elder, so I dutifully tried to figure out what she was saying. When she'd pause for a breath, I'd go get an adult to come translate for me. But sometimes from where her eyes landed in the kitchen, I could figure out she wanted something from the fridge or water from the sink. She'd smile when I got it right and say a phrase I wasn't accustomed to hearing even in English: "Gracias, mi amor."

Their mom—and matriarch of the house—was much younger than their grandmother and closer to Titi in age. She and Titi were probably sisters, but I can't be sure. I remember her being nice too. On Sundays, the entire apartment would fill with island flavors wafting from the kitchen. Sunday dinners were a big deal in the house, but the matriarch also sold pastelillos and pasteles to local neighbors, and Sunday was her main cooking day. I'd spend all day helping cut meat, stir sweet-smelling large metal pots on the stove, and carefully knot rope around banana leaves filled with savory meat and plantains mixed together.

I loved every minute of it except having to clean the chicken for the chicken-and-rice dish that would accompany dinner. The sink would be filled to the brim with chicken legs and wing carcasses. Using a butter knife, I'd peel back the skin and scrape away the slimy film and fat; globs of it would always stick to my fingers like glue. Their younger daughter and I would stand there for hours cleaning away and racing to see who could get done with their half of the pile fastest. It was hard work, but the tasty end results that I was allowed to eat with abandon made it worth it. A steady stream of knocks on the front door would come throughout the day with people stopping by to pick up their orders of pastelillos and pasteles or to place orders for the next week.

Us kids would take turns fishing labeled Ziplock bags of food out of the white rectangular deep freezer in the kitchen and bringing them to their mom to give to her customers.

Titi would stop by to visit us, and I would catch her giving their mom money from time to time. I'd only see my grandmother when Titi would take us back home to the apartment before the social worker came to visit. I'd be instructed not to tell the social worker we weren't staying at the apartment with my grandmother, and Titi never stuck around for the visits. After the social worker would leave, Titi would come back to collect us. I don't remember how long this deceit went on, but I remember Titi's family making me a birthday cake and going trick-or-treating in their building.

At some point, Titi and my grandmother had a fight, so my sister and I stopped living with Titi's vibrant family. Titi remained in the one-bedroom apartment, and my grandmother, sister, and I did not. Instead, we ended up apartment surfing through a flock of my grandmother's family members. We stayed with her cousins, uncles, and friends—usually a few nights at a time before moving on to a new place. Money exchanges for housing us were more blatant than when we stayed with Titi's family; with it being made clear to us that our welcome was contingent on my grandmother sharing her foster care payments. Without Titi to curb her cruel behavior, my grandmother went back to hitting me regularly, accusing me of stealing items from her and making me shrink in her presence.

During this period, when the State of New York believed I was living with my grandmother but in actuality I was being bounced around different homes, my attendance at school became especially sporadic. None of the places we stayed at were close to my school, and it seemed like it was a challenge for my grandmother to get anyone to take me there and pick me back up. I'm not sure why she couldn't take me herself, since I don't think she had a job, but that was not something I was crazy enough to ask her about. Nor was I delusional enough to ask who watched my sister during the day, since it seemed like my grandmother was always headed somewhere alone. Sometimes a random adult would take me to school on the subway, or sometimes by car, but I also remember the joy of being loaded onto someone's handlebars and being pedaled on a bike to school through the streets of New York. No, I didn't have a helmet, and I was too young to know I should have been afraid. I'll never forget how exciting the world seemed whizzing by.

Different people would pick me up in the evening and they rarely arrived on time. It didn't strike me as strange when one day after school, I stood on the corner of the Grand Concourse for an hour because no one had come to pick me up yet. I patiently waited three blocks away from my school, as my grandmother had instructed, as another three hours passed. My school building, which I could see in the light, disappeared from my sight. The blocks had faded to darkness, and I could no longer make out the familiar facades and doorways. It was late, I was alone, and I was suddenly scared. I thought about going back to the school to see if I could find a teacher to help me, but I was worried I'd get in trouble if I left the spot and was missed by whoever my grandmother sent to get me.

I waited a few minutes more and then walked to a payphone and called the only person I thought would help me and whose phone number I had memorized. Titi answered, and I told her no one had come to get me from school. With concern in her voice, she said, "Stay where you are, I'm on my way." A few minutes later, I watched as her figure got more defined in the dark as she quickly walked toward me. She took me back to the apartment, gave me something to eat, and went into the bedroom to call my grandmother. I couldn't make out what was being said since she closed the door and I was two rooms away in the kitchen, but from the raised tone of voice Titi was using, I knew it wasn't a good call.

I was finishing my homework when my grandmother arrived to pick me up. The two of them went into the bedroom to talk. When they emerged a while later, I could see Titi's eyes were red, and her cheeks looked damp. Hugs were given before my grandmother guided me out of the apartment, on the elevator, and into a cab where we rode silently to one of her friend's apartments for the night. My sister was already there, and I gave her a bottle and went to bed. After school the next day, I waited dutifully on the corner three blocks from my school when I heard Titi call my name. Her head was sticking out the passenger-side window of a white van. My grandmother and sister were inside. They waved me in, and we drove back to Titi's apartment where my clothes and schoolbooks were waiting.

We moved back in with Titi, and things were good again for my sister and me for a bit. My grandmother's worst impulses seemed to again be curbed with Titi around, and I didn't fear coming home to the apartment nearly as much. I'm not sure how long the reconciliation lasted in actuality, but it felt like a few months. Then one day I came home from school, and all of Titi's things were gone, and so was she. There was no goodbye, and the one time I asked after her, my grandmother told me, "Don't mention that name again." I knew Titi was ok; she had just decided not to stick around any longer, but my grandmother wanted to pretend she hadn't existed at all. I didn't have too much time to think about the loss because my grandmother became more unhinged with her attacks.

With the increase in violent outbursts also came an increase in surprises. I'd wake up to a gift of a new doll, dress, or toy that I'd be allowed to wear or play with, with the explicit instructions not to get it dirty or make noise. These gifts were surely meant to mollify me, but they had the opposite effect. One gift that caused me a lot of anxiety was a yellow dinosaur pin that she'd given me the morning of picture day.

The night before, she roughly woke me up to berate me for putting her gold lighter in my backpack. I hadn't—I was always too afraid of her to touch her things unless she told me to. Yelling at me, she insisted that I had stolen her lighter and put it in my bag. Crying, I kept denying it and reminded her that she had taken my backpack from me when I got home from school, and I hadn't been near it all evening. Instead of going to our babysitter's that day, she had instructed me to rush straight home from school because we were going out with some family members for dinner. She took my backpack as soon as I had walked through the door, and we turned around to leave for dinner soon after. We were out so late that I hadn't even done my homework, and she had told me to go to bed as soon as we returned home. I didn't say it, but I was also positive she had that fancy gold lighter in her hand when we were out to dinner.

Wet-faced, I stuck to my story that I couldn't have taken it, and her face softened for a moment. She leaned over me and said, "Well, if I ever catch you stealing anything I'll hold your hand over the stove burner and turn it on." Then she told me to go back to bed. The next day, I found a small, wrapped-in-paper jewelry gift box with the little yellow plastic dinosaur pin inside on top of my clothes that were laid out for picture day.

The dinosaur pin was really very cute, but it never made it into my photo. When I arrived at school, I found one of my classmates crying at breakfast. I don't remember why or if she had even told me the reason at all, but I remember pointing to my pretty dinosaur pin on my lapel and telling her she could borrow him for the day if she liked. She smiled and her tears subsided, and we ate our breakfast, giggled, and then got in line for class. I knew I'd need to get my pin back by the end of the day and wasn't worried about her not returning it. I didn't think about it again until I was in line to take my photo and suddenly realized that my grandmother would see in the picture prints that I hadn't worn the pin.

Fear swelled and then, just as quickly, it subsided. Wearing the pin made my classmate happy, and I wasn't going to take that away from her. No matter how scared I was of my grandmother, I liked the feeling of helping someone more. When it was my turn to take my photo, I posed and smiled as the camera flashed. Months later, I nervously handed my grandmother the sealed envelope of printed photos. My grandmother opened it, glanced at them, and went back to whatever she was doing. Relieved that she'd forgotten about the dinosaur pin, I went back to quietly doing my homework and trying to stay out of her way.

Years later, when my sister and I were officially out of foster care and reunified with my mom, Titi came for a visit to our little apartment in Harlem. I'm not sure my sister remembered her, since she was just a toddler the last time she saw her, but I did, and I was overjoyed. She took us out to lunch and a drive in her car. During the afternoon we talked about how I was doing in school and how we were adjusting to living with our mom.

Titi shared, too, about why she had left and not come back. I hadn't asked, but it seemed to just come pouring out of her. It really bothered her that she hadn't said goodbye. Apparently, living with my grandmother was simply hard on her mentally, and she couldn't take it anymore. I could understand that. She figured that my sister and I were good kids and would be ok in the end. Although I didn't understand the concept of closure, I was empathetic enough to respond with, "I understand." She drove us home sometime later and we never saw her again.

When I think about why my GG—in her twilight years, with her health failing—took me in, the answer quickly becomes clear. She was the one who cared, who could care, who wanted me to know I was worthy of being cared for. Because life is unfair. She wanted me to know a place where I was surrounded by kindness so that I could survive moments of heartlessness and not be weighed down by resentment. She took me in because she knew that once I knew what warmth felt like, no one—not strangers, not my family—could crush that part of me. Because pain can be passed down, she—and Titi—wanted me to know that cruelty was a choice and one I didn't have to choose. Kindness trumps fear, if we choose it. Even when it's just a dinosaur pin loaned to make a classmate smile. Love was the only shield my GG could offer me. And in the end, it proved to be enough.

I may not have had a perfect upbringing, but thanks to her, I learned that love and kindness are the most powerful forces in the world. They can transform pain into strength, loneliness into connection, and fear into hope. It's a lesson I carry with me every day, inspiring me to choose compassion and empathy, to be a light in the darkness for others, just as my GG was for me.

CHAPTER 4
Small Steps Forward

I CAN CLEARLY REMEMBER the day my grandmother unceremoniously dumped my sister and me back into foster care. I woke to find a large trash bag filled with our things sitting in the living room. Even before the knock on the door and the social worker entering the room, I knew what was happening. She collected my sister and me, and we walked past my grandmother sitting on her couch in her robe. I don't remember if my grandmother said goodbye, but I do remember the feeling of air filling my lungs after we departed the building lobby for the last time and walked outside.

We were dropped off at a foster home in one of the outer boroughs. It was a three-bedroom apartment in a small apartment building, but the neighborhood was filled with single- and two-family houses with flowers growing behind chain-link fences we'd walk past on the way to school. Our foster mom, a nurse who worked nights, had two bio kids: a daughter slightly older than me and a son who was in high school and would watch us while she was at work. She also had a foster care youth who was about a year old, a baby girl, who I'd learn from my quiet listening that she was trying to adopt. Even with her daughter, my sister, and me sharing a room—the baby girl slept in a crib in the mom's room, and her son had his own room—the apartment never felt tight. It was orderly, with her leaving a list of chores for us to complete while she was at work. A kitchen tidied before we went to bed would lead to us waking up to the smell of butter and pancakes in the morning. Dishes left in the sink would be met with cold cereal before being sent off to school.

All the kids would leave our homework out on the table for her to check before we headed off to school, and she'd jump through hoops to make sure we had what we needed for class projects. My sister and I had come to stay with her in the middle of the school year, and the class I was placed in was doing a play on what life was like in the 20th century for immigrants in New York City. The four things I remember most about this play were: how the teacher gave me three lines to say during the schoolwide assembly; how we sang "Getting to Know You," from *The King and I* ; how a classmate remarked I looked like "a rich immigrant" because my foster mom didn't have time to make me a costume and gave me a dress of hers to wear from her closet that dragged on the floor; and how my foster mom came to the play and gave me my first-ever bouquet of flowers when it was over. It wasn't the first school play I'd ever been in, but it was the first one for which I had someone in the audience cheering for me.

I liked living in that tidy three-bedroom apartment, but a few months after we arrived, I walked in the door from school to find my sister sitting next to a social worker on the couch and a large trash bag containing our things near the door.

Reunification with my mom took place around the end of my fourth-grade year of school. Her story is hers to tell, but somewhere along the way, she decided to prioritize my sister and me over her personal pain, to get clean and work to get custody of us back from the state. That courage is something that I would come to admire about my mother as I grew older and expanded my perspective. But it was not something that resonated with me deeply on the day the social worker surprise-moved my sister and me from a foster home where we were thriving to my mom's dark one-bedroom place in Harlem and just left us there.

I had always loved my mom and never once doubted that she loved me, but I didn't really have much to base that fact on, nor did I really know her all that well. I had seen her maybe once or twice a year during my time in foster care, and it was always during supervised visits. One of my favorite visits with my mother was a Christmas when she and one of her friends brought a large trash bag filled with presents for me to my social worker's office. I don't remember how long we actually visited, what gifts I got, or if I even got to keep any of them, but I remember feeling special that day.

Besides the infrequent visits, there had been the occasional letter I was forced to write to my mom from time to time, which I absolutely hated. I never knew what to say in those letters, so I always felt dread as I stared at the blank page. Truth be told, I actually had a better sense of what *not* to say in those letters, since whoever was in charge of me at the time—a foster parent, my questionably appointed guardian grandmother, a random adult who I'd been pawned off to without my social worker's knowledge—would read and critique them. Minutes would turn into hours as I grasped for words to fill the paper with graphite and, as I got older, ink. I was also very conscious of not wanting my mom to feel bad, so the end result was usually a single handwritten page of nothingness, updates devoid of relevance, for someone collecting a check to mail off.

More frequent over the years were our sporadic phone conversations that would take place every few months or so. Our conversations were never very long and about as groundbreaking as one could expect from an elementary-aged child who was keenly aware of the adult listening in nearby and the potential consequences of honesty. So, by the time my sister and I went to live with my mom, she and I were virtual strangers. All I had really been told about her was that she fought for us and wanted us—so I knew we were expected to want her too. No one asked me if I actually did. Like I said, I loved my mom—the way that all kids inherently love their mothers. But it felt like I was being thrown to live with her because we came from the same puzzle, when no one cared to confirm that the pieces actually fit.

Now a single mother of two, my mom enrolled in community college and worked a series of minimum-wage jobs that allowed her to move us from that darkly lit one-bedroom apartment where she slept on a pullout sofa in the living room to a slightly larger two-bedroom apartment. Some jobs required her to work through the night, others just extremely late into the evening. She had a series of meals that she'd make on repeat: lasagna, spaghetti Bolognese (which we knew as its less fancy name: "beef spaghetti"), and meatloaf with boxed potatoes. My mom would cook one of these each week in a large enough batch to get us through an entire week. Her lasagna was my favorite, and I could eat it for days on end—which is fortunate, because I did. After years of hustling between low-paying positions, she landed the extremely stressful but much better paying "good job" at OTB.

As the latchkey oldest, I spent my days continuing to watch over my younger sister, excelling at school and avoiding any trouble that I couldn't get myself out of. I had been placed on the "gifted" track early in my school career and maintained this status by the sheer grace of my teachers who would "unofficially" reassign me to the gifted class every time I bounced to a new school. It continued to be my foundation even when cracks I wasn't supposed to acknowledge started showing.

My mom and I had started to butt heads on things that might seem inconsequential to some but felt monumental to me. Arguments over curfews, homework, and clothing became battlegrounds for deeper issues of trust, independence, and the lingering effects of our past. Each disagreement was a reminder of the fragile balance we were trying to maintain, a dance around the blank pages of our history and the new life we were trying to build together. There was a push and pull for control which often led to me grasping tighter for independence. There was no huge eruption, just tiny tears that I felt pressure to maintain.

The truth is no one had prepared us for reunification. My mom was quick to change the subject whenever I would reference anything that happened before we were dropped off to live with her, so it became an unspoken weight between us. I spent a lot of time trying to smother my feelings, burying myself in books and signing up for extracurricular activities at school. Suddenly, I was expected to behave like a regular kid, but I'd spent most of my childhood in anything but a regular-kid role or environment. I was expected to trust my mom to "take care of things," but that didn't square with the fact that I was still responsible for looking after my sister like I had since the day I met her. I was supposed to believe that we were going to be fine, but I knew the reality was I could wake up to find a trash bag packed at the door at any time.

Worst of all, I felt guilty. Guilt for surviving foster care when so many other kids didn't. Guilt for receiving the "happy ending" of reunification and feeling anything but happy about it. Guilt for seeing my mom struggling to make it all work and still feeling like we never would.

It would take years for me to unpack all the feelings of confusion, guilt, and lingering trauma, but at that time I was determined to just keep moving forward. My mom was doing her best, so I would try to do my best too, even if it meant keeping my feelings to myself. Sometimes all we can do is do our best until we know what it will take to for us to do better.

CHAPTER 5
Right is Right

I HAD DETENTION ONLY once in my life, during my eighth-grade year of middle school. No longer in foster care, I had been "reunified" with my mom, and my sister and I had been living with her for three years. I was consistently tardy because my best friend, Tee, lived in the opposite direction of school. In my view, twenty blocks and one urine-scented elevator ride were a small price to pay for nonstop giggling and 13-year-old gossip while she got ready. We didn't typically even get out her door until 20 minutes after the school day started, but we never worried about anyone being upset with us for arriving late. We were incredibly good students, aced all our tests, participated in every class, took high school math and science on the weekends, and were in every club the school offered. Yes, even the boys' basketball team too.

Despite my minimal experience with basketball—having touched a basketball only three times in my life—my lack of athleticism in middle school didn't hinder our participation. Our on-court skills weren't essential for our role. Before each home game, the competing basketball teams had to answer a series of math problems to earn extra points and kick off the game. There was a limited time of about 10 minutes to solve these challenging equations, and Tee and I consistently worked together, getting all of them right before the other teams. Consequently, our team would gain a 10-point advantage on the scoreboard before the players even hit the court. It remains a mystery how two girls who didn't play basketball, didn't practice with the team, and didn't even have uniforms managed to compete in the boys' basketball academic challenge without anyone noticing.

The boys' basketball coach regularly invited us to the team's pizza party lunches. Naturally, we were more than happy to contribute to the team in the way we did. While I wouldn't go as far as to say that this made us above the rules, being ancillary members of the basketball team, academically inclined, and always willing to help our teachers made us be considered good kids. And good kids tended to get some breaks.

The other reason that we never worried about rushing to get to school was that Tee's mom would always write us a note excusing us from being late to class. The school's rule stated that if you had a note from your parents excusing your absence, you wouldn't be given detention. Tee's mom always included my name on her signed notes, so Tee and I would just hand them to the school officer on our way into school and head straight to homeroom. We never had a single issue arriving late until one day in early spring. On this sunny but very cold New York City day, the gym teacher happened to be checking late students in instead of the regular school officer. We walked in and Tee handed her our signed note. She read it and wrote our names in a spiral notebook like normal. But instead of telling us we could head to class, she looked at me and said, "Give me a smile."

Now, this wasn't the first time in my life that an adult had told me to "smile." As I grew older, I'd learn that I unequivocally have RBF—Resting Bitch Face. As a child and teen employee, people would couch their directive with "You look so much prettier when you smile," or "You don't look happy." No one ever seemed to care that in these moments when they were giving me unsolicited feedback on my appearance, I wasn't thinking about looking "prettier" or "happier"—I was just experiencing a comfortable moment being me.

My gym teacher continued to stare at me while holding our signed note. Maybe it was the fact that I was standing next to my first real friend, and I had watched for nearly two years how she carried herself with confidence, never once letting anyone look down on her. Or maybe after 13 years of adults telling me to smile and pretend to be happy, I'd had enough. Or maybe it was the fact that I was still bitter at this gym teacher for requiring students to buy a $10 school-branded T-shirt to wear to gym class, for which I was docked 30 points on my report card because I didn't have the money to buy the shirt in seventh grade. I'm not sure if it was one of these reasons that popped into my head as I blurted out, "I don't feel like smiling."

I never turned to look at her, but as I said those words, I could feel the smile creep across Tee's face. The gym teacher, clearly bothered, said, "Your friend can smile, and you can't?"

I didn't dare say, "She's not smiling for you." Instead, I stood there and stoically said, "I don't want to smile." She told Tee to go to class and told me she was going to make me stand by the wall until I smiled at her.

So, I stood.

A few teachers I knew passed through the doors and returned with coffee and brown bags stained with butter from the bodega across the street. My homeroom teacher was one of them. He stopped over at the check-in area to inquire why I was out of class. When he said hello, I happened to smile at him, which pissed the gym teacher off even more. She told him I was being "disrespectful" for not smiling at her and clearly, I knew how to smile, since I smiled at him. My homeroom teacher shook his head and told her that keeping me here had caused me to miss the standardized reading test and that I'd have to make it up. She told him that when I smiled at her, I could go.

So, I stood. For two hours.

The school officer came to relieve the gym teacher from the check-in desk. The gym teacher, not to be defeated by an eighth grader, handed me a detention slip and told me I'd have detention until I learned to smile but I could go to class. Stone-faced and without a word, I took the slip from her hand and headed up the stairs to class. As I walked through my homeroom door, I balled up the dentition slip and threw it in the trash.

So, that day when school ended, I stood—and walked away, all the way back to Tee's house, without a care.

It's not that I wasn't afraid of getting in trouble. My mom, who I had been reunified with by this time, had no clue that I was late to school pretty regularly. I actually left our apartment with more than enough time to get to school on time. She just had no idea that on some mornings when I headed out the door I was going to Tee's house and Tee's mom was just letting us be late to school, giving us signed notes so we didn't get detention. My mom was pretty hands-off when it came to me because as far as she knew all I did was go to school, get good grades, hang out with smart girls in my class, and take care of my sister. She would have been upset to find out that I was making up my own school hours. But I wasn't worried about her finding out about that because I knew that's all she would have been upset with me about.

Our relationship wasn't a traditional mother/daughter relationship since I had spent much of my childhood in foster care. My mom was figuring out how to be a single parent and dealing with all the stress of having two kids under her care while holding down an overnight job, but with everything going on I learned early on that my mom was a very measured person. Life was black and white to her. Dozens of times I heard her counsel her friends on the phone: "Right is right and wrong is wrong."

My showing up to school late was wrong. But a teacher holding me outside of class and making me miss a required standardized test because I didn't smile for her? That was more wrong. And that same gym teacher giving me detention, not because I was late, but because I refused to smile, was even more wrong. I knew my skipping detention would be looked at as right by my mom. So, I wasn't too worried about her finding out. I'll even go so far as to say, I wish that gym teacher would have called. It would have been a wake-up moment for her.

But she never did, and I never stepped foot in detention. I would see her in gym class each week and pass her in the halls, but she never spoke a word to me the rest of the year. I think, in the end, she realized that she was wrong and decided just ignoring me was the best course of action. I wasn't the type of kid to stir up trouble, so with the exception of purposely never smiling wherever I saw her, I was fine to coexist with the tension. Years within the foster care system and its aftermath had made me comfortable with being uncomfortable. It's a way of being that would go on to serve me well.

CHAPTER 6
Find a Court of Your Own

I WASN'T SUPPOSED TO like tennis. It just wasn't a sport that popped to the top of the list of available childhood activities for a poor kid growing up in Harlem. And, of course, I wasn't supposed to be *good* at tennis. I had only swung a racket once in my life, and that was during a YMCA field day trip when I was in second or third grade. I don't remember if I even made contact with the ball. And I most definitely wasn't supposed to be able to win tennis matches.

I only joined my high school team because all students were required to take a spring athletic activity, and I happened to have an old hand-me-down racket my godmother gifted me when she found out I received a scholarship to boarding school. Up until this point in my life, I had always been walking forward towards an undefined "better life." I didn't know what that "better life" would entail, but I was certain the way to obtain it was to do things differently than my family, than my foster parents and all the questionable adults I had known. That meant doing well in school, signing up for before- and after-school programs, and joining every free weekend program I came across. School was the only ticket I had for the road to a "better life," so when the opportunity for a scholarship to attend a $20,000-a-year boarding school in Arizona presented itself—I said yes. I had been reunified with my mom for a little over three years by this point and considered this no different than all the other moves I'd made in my life. I thought it would be an adjustment, but I was woefully unprepared for how hard entering a new world would be.

I found myself 2,000 miles away from home, on the tennis team, loving a sport that I was good enough at to win against players who assumed they'd be much better than me. Sometimes the unexpected leaves the biggest impact on our lives. Tennis was that way for me. It gave me a new way to breathe when the air around got to be so thick, I stopped wanting to inhale.

If I were writing a sitcom script, it'd be hard to find a place more opposite from Harlem than where I went to high school. For one, it was a working cattle ranch: cows, horses, and more nature per square foot than I'd ever spent much time with. For another, students there were rich. Not "more money than Harlem" rich. Rich *rich.* Fly strawberries to you on our private plane because they're your favorite, rich.

It wasn't just a culture shock; it was a reality whiplash. Before I stepped foot on campus, I never realized how much I didn't actually have. This was a place where newly licensed teens got luxury cars for their 16th birthday, went summering in Europe and skiing when it snowed. I'd only seen that type of lifestyle lived in TV shows, and I had been too young and naïve to know that it was an actual reality for other kids. More overwhelming to me, especially on arrival day, were the families themselves. Moms and dads accompanied their kids to the campus to drop them off and help them get settled. Some parents flew in to help their kids move into their dorm room and hang posters on their walls. The school had sent a campus van to pick me and a few international students up at the airport. It had been my first time on a plane, and I somehow managed to lug my oversized duffle bag through the airport and to the van by myself. I don't think I've ever felt more alone than I did standing at the end of the walkway of girls' dorms with my duffle slid behind me as I watched all the kids and their parents.

School had never been hard for me, but that first semester of boarding school was. You wouldn't have known it from my grades, though. I consistently made the honor roll and managed to win awards for my work in history class. But mentally, I struggled. The first week of school I was able to find a job at the on-campus convenience store. I desperately needed to work since my scholarship only covered educational expenses and didn't cover other things a teen girl needed, like toothpaste, tampons, and detergent to do my laundry. Most of my fellow students had parents who sent them money or had their own credit and debit cards to get things themselves. That wasn't an option for me. Because I was a freshman, I was only allowed to work a few hours a week at the convenience store, so I also started babysitting for a few of my teachers' kids.

All the teachers lived in on-campus housing, and a number of them had young children. I'd been watching kids all my life, from my baby sister to other babies in the foster homes I was placed in, so I was pretty adept at keeping little ones safe, clean, and entertained. I'd babysit on the weekends while other students were taking trips to the mall or going for overnight stays with friends who had homes locally. Every once in a while, I'd have enough money to pay the $15 fee for a weekend van trip to the movies or mall, but it was really rare that I could cover the cost. For most of my first semester, if I wasn't working or studying, I was reading books borrowed from the campus library, crying, or sleeping. I did the latter two a lot.

Part of my stress was caused by the pressure of having to work and get good grades to maintain my scholarship. More of it was caused by unfamiliarity with the cultural nuances of my new environment. Every student was assigned a teacher advisor, and their advisees—a group of six to eight students—would spend one evening a week at their house to hang out and talk. We'd also have a weekly formal sit-down dinner together in the dining hall. I'd never done a sit-down dinner before attending boarding school, let alone a formal one, and too many years in foster care made me leery of being in my advisor's home—even with other students there. Every interaction was so unnerving and made me question everything I'd experienced in my life up to that point. There were mandatory curfews, study halls, and camping trips; room inspections, set eating times, and Vespers; dogs that roamed the campus freely, rigid schedules, and athletic activity requirements; community service mandates, honors lists, and adult expectations at every turn. Those first months at boarding school made me unsteady. Everything I believed suddenly seemed wrong, and everything that kept me grounded felt unpredictably breakable.

All of this was compounded by certain students making my daily life a living hell and my not knowing how to deal with it. You can place the types of students who attend boarding school into two general categories. There is the "opportunistic set": those who attended or were convinced to attend because doing so would provide additional opportunities in life like getting into a good college or making or furthering connections that would impact their future employment, financial status, friends and acquaintances, or marriage prospects. This makes up a majority of the students on campus—the legacies, the athletes, the scholarship kids, the overachievers, the straight-and-narrows.

The second category of students—although much smaller—is a pretty identifiable group as well. This is the "no alternative set": made up of those who attend because they are forced to or have no other options—the previously suspended or expelled, the addicted or recovering, the last stop before military school, the family disappointments and hide-aways. Years of personal therapy and trauma-informed work with unfairly labeled foster youth as an adult would awaken my realization that the "no alternative set" at my school were just pained teens acting out to mask their cries for help. But that compassionate awareness was hard to see when my tormentors were among them.

First there was my heavy drug-using roommate and her "gang member" bestie who claimed to be part of either the Bloods or Crips (I can't remember which one). To be fair to my roommate, she was nice enough to offer me some of her cocaine and acid on the first day we met, but I think my quick—and possibly judgmental—rejection of her overture drew the lines of conflict between us. Alone, she wasn't that bad, but when she was with her friends, they were awful. I'd come back from class, and they'd have eight girls in our small dorm room getting high and listening to loud music. They had their drugs shipped to them and it felt like there was an unending supply that arrived every week. They would "borrow" my things, and I'd have to hunt them down around campus to get them back. They would also make fun of me for things like my taste in music—I leaned toward R&B and showtunes over rap—and the fact that they were "Blacker" than me since they had more Black friends on campus than I did.

In an attempt to push back on their imposing behavior, I told them to stop taking my stuff and keep their "guests" out of my side of the room, but my roommate's friend told me there was nothing I could do about it. It wasn't a particularly nuanced threat. I knew she was right, so I took to avoiding being in my dorm room until curfew each evening. It's not that I was scared of a physical altercation with them: I'm no prize fighter, but had I held my own when I had to in Harlem. It's that this wasn't Harlem, and they were rich and White and set up to get their way. I was one of 10 Black students—all scholarship kids from "disadvantaged" areas. They knew they held the upper hand and that there was truly nothing I could do about it. My attempts to evade my tormentors by staying out of my room might have been more impactful if I didn't have another bully waiting at the ready whenever I stepped out.

This girl—let's call her Brenda—was older, popular, rich, and blond… and seemed to take immense pleasure in making fun of the fact that I was none of those things. Her favorite refrain was to call my clothes cheap and say I was from the ghetto in front of her friends. Both statements were true, but they never caused me shame before she started voicing them, like pronouncements of judgements. She'd talk about me with her friends circling her, whispering loud enough for me to overhear her cruel comments and their laughs. One time, someone in her group noticed I was in earshot—and, not fully understanding the depths of her intentions, told her I could hear them. She turned, looked at me scornfully, and simply said, "So what?" in response.

It's not like I hadn't encountered racism before I stepped foot on that boarding school campus. I was seven or eight the first time an adult called me the "N" word. I was in a foster parent's car, and we were waiting for some woman to pull out of a parking spot. The woman was talking with someone—a friend, probably—and I guess she didn't like that we pulled up near her car to wait for the spot. So, as she got in her car, she called us a bunch of "Ns" before she closed her car door. My foster parent just laughed it off.

I was even younger when a foster parent had sent me to buy milk from a bodega a few blocks away. The owner searched my backpack before he'd let me leave the store because he assumed I had stolen something—I hadn't. I was a bit older and in middle school when a worker followed me and my friends around a prom shop at the mall on 34th Street. We weren't being loud at all. We were just killing time, looking at fun dresses, but we instinctively knew we should just leave before the worker caused any trouble. Although those indignities left lasting scars, they could be ignored in the immediate, even compartmentalized away because the moments were temporary.

But there is absolutely no reprieve when you live and go to school with your oppressors. I found myself suffocating in place, feeling more miserable each day but still getting all my classwork, required activities, and work-work done. When my roommate wasn't around or went off-campus for the weekend, I'd spend all day in bed, usually skipping meals so I could avoid seeing anyone. The first half of the school year continued on, and these coping mechanisms led to my feeling absolutely hopeless. It felt as if no one wanted me around and no one would miss me if I weren't—not just at boarding school, but back home as well. My many years of foster care and constant abuse were still open wounds that were raw and unaddressed, and being relentlessly bullied at school left me feeling like hurt was the only thing out in the world for me. No matter how hard I tried to learn, get good grades, and stay out of trouble, life just kept finding a way to punish me and show me that none of my work mattered.

I wish I could have put these feelings into clearer words. Finally, towards the end of Christmas break, I broke down as I was packing my things to go back to boarding school. Through tears, I blurted out to my mom, "I don't want to go back to boarding school." She asked me why and all my teen brain could muster was, "I don't like it there."

I was years from understanding the latent trauma caused by my time in foster care, my functioning depression and anxiety caused by my on-campus bullies, and my suicidal thoughts caused by the stressors and pressure of my life. For all the pain I was feeling, I had no better way to express myself, but it's impossible to tell someone you're drowning when you're already submerged under water. My mom, not having a good handle on what I was experiencing—or a way to coax it out of me—simply said, "You have to go back." And that was that.

The six-hour plane ride I took alone the next day was a blur and I was numb for the entire trip and much of the start of the second semester. Everything continued along in a haze, with me feeling increasingly alone, unsettling thoughts creeping more frequently into my mind. I found myself withdrawing even more and found it harder to hide my anger, not just from my teachers but from myself, too.

One of my teachers, Becky Butcher, noticed my despondent demeanor and began taking a highly active interest in trying to help me settle in more on campus. I liked Becky from the moment I met her. She wasn't like the other teachers on campus. Speaking to her just once let you know that she lived life on her own terms, and she simply wasn't going to take a mess from anyone. She smoked without shame. She was a walking thesaurus but could just as effortlessly call someone a "shithead" without missing a beat. She could talk just about anyone off a ledge. And she had a knack for taking care of strays—both cats that would pop up around campus and students who didn't quite fit in.

Since Becky wasn't my sanctioned teacher advisor, she couldn't just pull me into her advisee group, so she began by including me in her ancillary activities—things like movie nights or weekend dinners at her house with other students she'd taken under her kindly wings.

I ended up becoming friends with her son Nick, who was a grade or two older. We bonded over our shared love of Disney musicals, Broadway soundtracks, and satirical comedy TV shows. He had a kind heart and a strong confidence about who he was and the things he loved. He radiated so brightly. Nick introduced me to some of his kindhearted friends who became my lifeline. There was Cy, who helped me strategize probably the most complicated but approved multi-student room switch in the school's history, making me her roommate and ending my time feeling like a captive in the dorm. There was also Susie, who had grown up at the school because her parents were teachers and who knew all the fun places to hide out on campus. We'd spend hours talking about nothing and everything and watching movies on the TV she had in her dorm room. She and I quickly became close friends.

I became even closer to a friend I had made earlier in the year—Kelly. She was a scholarship kid too. She was sweet, loved horses, and didn't make fun of me when I held on too tightly to the saddle horn, afraid of falling off during trail rides. Kelly was nice in a refreshing and honest way, and I always felt happier when she was around. With the expansion of my friend circle, things got a little better for me. Suddenly I had more positive outlets—more people to laugh with and just relax around. Even with that, I didn't tell my friends about the bullying. Just like my hiding of my foster care background from them, there were some things I wasn't comfortable sharing with anyone, and part of me believed that I just had to suffer through it—that it was just part of life. Keeping people, even friends, at a distance had kept me safe for so long; I wasn't ready to take the risk that they might not understand or would treat me differently. I didn't want and wasn't ready to be judged, so I stayed silent.

But in spite of my hesitation to speak up, life did start to get easier. Once I moved dorm rooms, I'd only encounter my old roommate and her friend in one-offs around campus. That became a nonissue as well once they either got expelled or withdrew from the school. I don't remember the exact details but remember murmurs of "drugs being found" and then they were no longer at school. Encounters with my upperclassman tormentor became less intense around this time as well. It might have had something to do with the fact that some of my new friends were upperclassmen too and might not have been too keen to look the other way at her outright cruelty. She was still awful, but she would refrain from uttering any comments to me when I was around friends who were her peers. I took her calculated reticence as a win, although her insults stung just as badly when they were lobbed without an audience.

With some of the haziness parting around me, I found myself needing to select a spring sport to occupy my afternoons. I had signed up for whatever free activity was offered for fall but had a harder time selecting one for the back half of the school year. My school required all students to sign up for an athletic activity for each semester and although there were a few to choose from, none really appealed to me. Becky recommended I try out for softball, which she coached. I considered it until I found out I'd have to buy a glove, knee pads, and other items to outfit myself for the team. My lack of funds basically shut out any sport that would require hefty purchases of shoes or gear like softball, track, or rock climbing.

But I happened to have that used tennis racket my god-mom had gifted me and already owned sneakers, a beat-up old pair of black Reeboks, so I joined the tennis team. I did have to buy a white tennis skirt, but I found one for $15 at a thrift shop. It was four sizes too big for me. I safety-pinned it.

It was the first time I had played on a competitive team and had an actual "coach." Most of the students on my team had grown up playing tennis and were all relatively good at the sport. I, on the other hand, was a complete novice and had to learn every aspect of the game while prepping for our first match day. Luckily, my teammates were amazingly kind and would take the time to show me how to swing correctly or let me try again if I completely missed a ball or made an error. It also helped a lot that I seemed to have some natural talent for the game and was able to execute on the lessons my coaches shared really quickly. I went from knowing nothing about tennis to winning my first competitive match about four weeks later.

Tennis became my safe space very quickly. I'd rush back to my dorm room to quickly change after class and be the first one on the court for practice. I started playing on the weekends and would spend hours hitting with teammates or just working on my serve. If the coach said I needed to work on a foot movement or a swing or pacing, I'd work on it relentlessly until I perfected it. The more I practiced and played, the more at ease I started to feel not only on the court but in my body and in my life. On the court there was no room for doubt, and being mad only led to unforced errors. I couldn't carry my anger onto the court; I had to lay it down if I wanted to play well and win. Somewhere out on that tennis court I decided that I liked the confident person I was when I played more than I disliked feeling broken. My mentality flipped. And the more I won, the harder it was to feel like I needed to keep carrying that broken version of me around.

Having teammates rooting for me to win and me rooting for them was a new experience for me as well. During competitions, if we were between matches, we'd make a beeline to watch our friends play and cheer them on. Yes, hearing loud claps feels incredible when you've made a great shot, but so does hearing a supportive "you've got this" after making a bad one.

Learning to play with a partner was a new social skill for me too.

Playing doubles meant I had to be in sync with my partner. I had to learn how she moved and thought, and more importantly I had to trust her to know how I moved and thought as well. We had to understand each other's limitations—where we were weak—and be open with each other so we could close our gaps. I had to fill in where my partner was weak, and she had to do the same for me.

Like on her backhand. My partner was a stellar player and had been playing since she was a child, but her backhand left a lot to be desired, especially that first season we played together. When she hit a backhand, the ball would sometimes soar out or even slam into the net. As soon as our opponents caught wind, they would smartly try to send balls just to her backhand to try to get her to make an unforced error, giving them the point. Tennis is a game of strategy, after all. But they usually hadn't factored in my sister-like, overprotective nature when it came to my friends. Picking on her was just not allowed. As soon as I'd see them setting up to hit a crosscourt shot to her backhand, I'd be ready to poach the ball at the net for the unexpected return. Nine times out of ten, we'd win the point, and they'd always hesitate to try and force a backhand swing to my partner again.

It was the same way with me, especially with my pathetic second serve. My first serve was pretty strong, and I had a lot of control over where I wanted the ball to land, but my consistency was far from perfect. Whenever I had to take a second serve, I'd opt to hit a safe, slow shallow ball to avoid double faulting. The issue with slow, shallow second serves is that any receiving player worth their salt is going to try to win the point with a fast down-the-line, a short crosscourt, or a deep crosscourt return because they can control the pace of play. The deep crosscourt shot is always the safer play since there is less room for error, but a good or cocky player will go for a short or a down-the-line alley shot. For anyone foolish enough to try for those, my partner was ready to make them regret their overzealous decision with a beautifully deep crosscourt volley winner. They'd usually choose the safer return on second serves the rest of the match.

As much as playing doubles taught me to trust the people pulling for me, playing singles taught me to trust myself. Tennis is supposed to be a "gentleman's game," a sport for "civilized people," but that is just a coded way of saying that people who look like me aren't supposed to play it. There are myriad unspoken barriers to entry, like the fact that you're supposed to wear all white to compete (requiring additional cleaning costs), or the fact that tennis courts require a lot of space and are notoriously difficult to maintain (meaning they're more likely to be found in wealthier areas). Then there are the direct obstacles, like the players who would accuse me of cheating or would cheat themselves, and their adult coaches who would call me the "N" word or "Black B" under their breath. I was out of my depth in knowing how to handle most of the cruelty I encountered in my early months of boarding school, but as luck would have it, I was about to receive a roadmap.

Around the same time I fell in love with playing tennis, I also fell in love with an incredible sister duo from Compton who were dominating professional tournaments across the globe—the Williams sisters. Whenever I could commandeer the TV in the student lounge to watch Venus and Serena play, I would, and I read every online news article I could find that mentioned their name. Some of the articles would simply recount their wins or talk about their incredible rise from the south side of LA to playing on the biggest courts in the world. But many of the articles would take swipes at them somewhere in the prose. So many writers criticized the girls for being "classless" because they wore their hair in braids with colorful beads or "unfeminine" because of how their skirts fit on their curvier bodies. Commentators would make underhanded comments calling the girls' style of playing "uncivilized" or "aggressive" because of the intense power of their swing or how they stood tall on the court. Reporters implied that their matches must have been "fixed," and therefore the girls were "cheaters" because they won so often.

The more the Williams sisters racked up wins, the more insulting and personal the criticisms became. Of course, beauty and luxury companies wouldn't want to hire them for brand deals because their look was "non-traditional." And, when Venus and Serena were the only two competitors left standing in tournament after tournament after dominating in the sport, they went as far as to label the girls "unexciting," indicating that no one would want to see the sisters play against each other.

I watched, read, and listened to grown adults lob all this bitterness and cruelty at these two young girls because they simply dared to be great at tennis while Black. And I watched how the sisters responded. They didn't clap back. They didn't say unkind things in return. They just kept playing and winning and smiling every time they did. I was too young and secluded in my own struggles to realize the revolutionary impact that the Williams sisters were having on the world, but I was fully aware of their impact on me. How they played was how I wanted to play, how they acted was how I wanted to act, and so I decided to model their behaviors on the court in every way I could. Perhaps I couldn't match their playing style—those girls were and are in a league of their own—but I definitely could in spirit and attitude.

When an opponent would accuse me of wrongly calling one of their balls out, I'd smile and say, "Let's play the point again." When a coach would call me an unsavory name under their breath, I'd look their way, shake my head *no*, and go back to whatever I was doing. When it was clear that an opponent was calling line shots I knew were in as "out," I'd change my game and hit shorter shots that couldn't be questioned. I'd smile when I'd made good shots and make a note to correct myself when I made bad ones. If I was having a hard moment on court, I'd think about what Venus and Serena would do, and then I'd just continue to play my game. Tennis gave me confidence, but it was the Williams sisters who molded my character, and I wielded it like a shield. In four years of playing on my high school team, I'd only lose one competitive singles match. It's incredible how hard it is to feel less than when you're winning—how hard it is to internalize other people's vile words when you know the one word they really want to call you, "loser," is the one word they can't.

Over time, my confidence began to improve beyond the court as well. The growth was more gradual, but with each high school year that passed, I became more comfortable in my own skin. The fear of standing up for myself became less pronounced, and to some of my peers' and teachers' chagrin, I became better at not always opting out of voicing my concerns. Crucially, I learned the value of keeping my friends close, forming bonds that became pillars of support. And, equally important, I discovered that I genuinely liked the person I was becoming. My shame and angst from all my traumas didn't disappear, but the prospect of living life on my own terms filled me with hope. It took a game that uses "love" as a basis of scoring to help me realize that my own self-love was required for me to be able to move forward in life. I had to break the idea that I was a zero and just put points on the board. For the first time in a long time, I was excited to embrace the journey of self-discovery that was in front of me, and while challenges would always be there, I was grateful to be alive to meet them as they came.

CHAPTER 7
Love Is a Verb

My mom's office was unnervingly quiet as we walked through the halls. The call center was a stone's throw away from a half-dozen dimly lit elevators that opened to a dark hallway in an eye-strainingly tall but unassuming building at the heart of Times Square. Being a junior in college, I had been to her job before when I was home on breaks, and it was always filled with loud and energetic voices answering phones, placing bets, and confirming orders. The decibels from the usual commotion could rival any noise taking place out in the streets below, but today they felt muted, reduced.

My mom was a phone operator for Off Track Betting (OTB)—a betting house for racehorses in New York City. It was a job she landed after my sister and I exited foster care and lived with her. It was a union job that I had come to understand was stressful but paid pretty well. Phone operators spent their shifts obsessively ensuring that they correctly captured phone bets from hectic, excited, or panicked gamblers because mistakes were very costly. Winning bet amounts that were captured incorrectly by operators were deducted directly from their paychecks to compensate bettors. My mom told me about a co-worker who made a $40,000 error. He quit the same day rather than being forced into a repayment plan that would garnish a substantial portion of his wages for the foreseeable future.

While my mom had made a few mistakes placing bets over the years, none were as devastatingly high as $40,000. I knew from her stories that there was nothing worse for her team than one of them being called into their supervisor's office to listen to a playback recording of a bet they'd placed for a customer. It was customary for operators to preemptively ask, "How much?" before they even sat down, so they could determine if it was worth listening to the playback at all or just quit on the spot. The stakes were always high in that place, and tension was consistently in the air.

But today it was stifling.

In all, I only lived with my mom for about four or five years during my adolescence. Five years might sound like a lot of time, but it's just shy of one-third of the time most kids spend with their moms before graduating middle school. Of course, I would head back "home" for school holidays and summer breaks during boarding school and college, but going back to that two-bedroom apartment never really felt like home. Maybe it was because of all the moving I had done in foster care, the constant shuffling from strange place to strange place every few months—or sometimes, within days. Four walls don't make a house a home any more than blood makes someone truly family. It was with all of this unrequested insight walled up inside of me that during winter break, I found myself being led by my mother through the maze of cubicles and women on phones on her work floor. The energy was off, but I tried to ignore it as she escorted me into the conference room. I was there to receive a scholarship award of $500 as the winner of the OTB's company essay contest for college students. I was always a fairly good writer and had won the contest in the two prior years as well.

Even with the lingering tension I was excited to collect this award, and the presentation was a very civil and fast affair. A representative for OTB handed me the check and smiled awkwardly as he shook my hand. We posed for a photo, and I made sure to thank everyone in the room. They, in turn, told me how much they enjoyed my essay. The entire event was completed in 15 minutes or so. My mom needed to swing by her desk to grab her work ID so she could escort me upstairs to cash the check at their internal teller. I had already earmarked that prize money to cover part of my spring semester textbooks, so there was absolutely no need to even think about depositing it into my checking account and waiting for the money to clear. And I knew from my previous award visits that the OTB internal teller would cash the check for free for me, so it made sense to do this all while I was there.

While we were at my mom's desk, one of the co-workers that my mom was friendly with happened to end her call and scooted over in her chair to say, "Hi." I'd met her before, so we chatted while my mom unlocked her drawer to grab her purse.

"Congratulations."

"Thank you," I said politely.

"Girl, your mama almost had a riot going on in here. Did she tell you?"

I stammered out, "Uh, no."

"Those fools told your mom they were going to give that award money to someone else this year because you'd already won it twice."

Confused, I looked over at my mom, and she stared me right in the eyes as she said, "They told me your essay was the best, but they were going to give it to someone else to make it fair. I told them it wasn't fair if they weren't going to give the award to the kid that wrote the best essay."

"She did more than that," her co-worker cackled. "She—"

My mom cut her off and told her we needed to hurry upstairs before her break was over. Waving goodbye, as we walked, I understood the stolen glances that shot our way as we made our way back through the buzzing but tense office floor and out into the dark hallway to wait for the elevator. Upstairs, the teller cashed my prize check, said, "Congratulations," and handed me my $500 in cash. My mom walked me back to the elevator bank, told me she'd see me at home, and sent me on my way.

To this day, I have no idea about the level of fury that my mother rained down on "those fools." Did she blackout on them and make them regret the day they were born? That would have been a sight.

Did she explain the flaw in their logic, as casually as she had to me by her desk? You know, possibly making them shrink in their absurdity? *Perhaps.*

Did she really rally her entire office to threaten to strike—or riot, as her co-worker implied? I have seen streaks of both Norma Rae and

Rosa Parks peek out in my mother over the years, especially as she's gotten older.

Did she calmly suggest that her union rep should take a peek at their review process for awarding winners? That would have been both an utterly strategic and savage move. I wouldn't put it past her.

I honestly have no idea what approach she took and have never asked. It's become another one of those unspoken truths in our relationship and has added to the magical mystique of my mother over the years. Not knowing what she did sits right with me. Just knowing that she did it—chose to fight for me when I did not even know a battle was being waged—is more than enough.

It should shock no one to learn that I did not win the essay award again the following year. As it turns out, getting told about yourself—or whatever approach my mother took—was enough to inspire the one-billion-dollar gambling company to fold its hand and slither away from the contest altogether. It wasn't held the next year, or ever again from what I understand. Apparently, you can't beat the house, but you can shake it to its core.

Isn't that the power of love, after all? That inconspicuous force that radiates with enough energy to move mountains? My mother showed me that love is not only a force but also an action we choose every day. When we choose love, we choose to care, to try, to fight, to repair, to not give in. Life is filled with obstacles, pains, and demons that will bring us to our knees. This is the reality for every single person on this earth. But we get to make the choice—we have to choose—to rise through the pain, to heal where we can, to fight for what and who we love. And that choice is no one's but yours to make.

That two-bedroom apartment would never come to feel like home for me. But, years later, when I went on to create a home of my own, I knew what I wanted it to feel like. There was a foundation there, thanks to my mom. I wanted it to feel stable, safe, and secure—the things I didn't feel when I was a child. And I also wanted it to be filled with love, the kind that you choose to choose each day. So, I wasn't starting from scratch as I set out to create one filled with both.

CHAPTER 8
Protect Your Peace

I BOARDED A PLANE to London with $200 in my bank account. It was my first international flight, and, in a few hours, I'd step foot for the first time in a new country. I hadn't planned to study abroad for the last semester of my senior year of college, but I'd found the courage to take the risk and go for it. As the plane glided over the Atlantic, practical worries lingering in the back of my mind—like how I was going to be able to survive for six months with only $200 to my name—were silenced by the excitement of me stepping out to see the world on my terms. This wasn't my first attempt at trying to expand my horizons, but it was the first time I did so with nothing holding me back.

Back when I was in boarding school, a woman came to campus and gave a really cool presentation on a Russian study abroad program for high school students. The program took place during the summer, and students toured different cities throughout the country for a few weeks, immersing themselves in the culture and communities. I had never thought much of traveling outside of the United States, except for my secret desire to go to Paris one day and see the Eiffel Tower. That dream was inspired by my love of the movie *Funny Face*, starring Audrey Hepburn, which I had watched during the summer when one of my foster parents refused to let us kids go outside at all. In the movie, her dream is to go to Paris, and she begrudgingly accepts a job as a fashion model because it will get her there. The way she described the city and the way it appeared in the film made the place look like pure magic. Russia was a long way from France, but the program director made it sound like a pretty amazing place to see as well.

After the presentation, I stayed behind the group of students that made their way out of the room and asked the woman how much the program cost. I don't remember exactly how much she said, but it was in the thousands, and I knew there was no way I could ever afford it. She gave me her card and told me to reach out to her if I was interested in going. I took it, knowing this was probably the last time that I would speak to her.

A few days later, I was on the phone with my grandmother—the one who had fostered my sister and me before turning us back over to the state. Now that we were reunified with my mother, I was required to have a relationship with her mother as well. She was the family matriarch, and she wanted me to call her regularly. To not do so would have created problems for my mother, and I wasn't one to stir the pot. So, I tried to call regularly to keep the peace.

I needed something to talk about on our bimonthly awkward calls, so I usually just recounted what I did that week to fill the time. So I told her about the Russian presentation. Usually, her responses to things I shared were, "That's nice," or "That's good," but when I mentioned the Russia study abroad, she asked if other students were going. I said, "Yes, I think some signed up." She asked if I wanted to go. I said, "Yes, but it is really expensive, and I don't have the money to go."

Without missing a beat, she said, "*If* you come up with half the money, I'll give you the other half." My heart jumped a beat. Coming up with half the money was still an impossible task, but half was better than all. I was so excited and couldn't believe she would do that for me. I thanked her and after we hung up started thinking about ways to make the money I needed. I knew I wouldn't be able to work enough to get it—there weren't enough hours in the day, and I only made a few dollars an hour anyway. I couldn't ask my mom for the money since I knew she didn't have it. I had no idea how I could come up with the cash, but I figured I should let the director of the program know that

I was at least interested and find out when the deadlines were to pay for a spot.

When I got her on the phone, she was genuinely happy for me. I told her my grandmother said that she'd pay for half the trip if I could come up with the other half, but I wasn't sure I could. I shared that my family didn't have a lot of money, that I was a scholarship kid and although I worked on campus, I didn't make anywhere near enough to cover the rest of the cost. She said that she could help me since I was at the school on a scholarship. She told me the program had donors who would pay for some of the trip fees for students in need. She would need me to write an essay on why I would benefit from being a part of the program and how it would impact my life, and once she had it, she would see if she could get some of her donors to help.

I was a fairly good essay writer and could think of lots of ways that studying in Russia would positively benefit my education and knowledge of the world. I got to work on it immediately and asked my English teacher to help me edit it. I submitted it about a week later and then waited to hear back from the program director. A few weeks later, I got a page over the school intercom system that I had a call waiting for me in the reception building. I hurried over to answer, and it was the program director on the line with the news that she had a donor who was willing to sponsor half the cost of the trip for me. My heart swelled. I couldn't believe that a stranger would be so kind and generous. I thanked her so many times. Downplaying her efforts, she just responded, "I'm happy to help," and then told me when the rest of the money would be due and when the final itinerary would be shared. When we got off the phone, I rushed to call my grandmother and tell her the amazing news.

It was the middle of the week, and I usually called over the weekends, so I think I caught her off guard when she answered the phone. Excitement took over, and I'm quite sure I blurted out that I had enough money to go on the Russian trip, and that the program director had found the funds for me. Smiling through the phone, I started to tell my grandma the details of when the rest of the money would be due, but she cut me off. "Your aunt has HIV, so I need to help her with her medical bills now. So, I won't be able to give you money for the trip."

I couldn't breathe. For everything I had heard and read about HIV—about how it wasn't transmissible by touch or saliva or sweat, and that people with it can live long lives with treatment—all I could think was *I don't want my aunt to die.* I can't remember anything that my grandmother said after that or even leaving the reception building. I just remember standing outside my dorm room crying alone, feeling terrified that my aunt was going to die. Devastated, I walked aimlessly between the dorm paths, my face wet with tears, and ran straight into Nick, the upperclassman who had befriended me the year earlier. Immediately, he embraced me and asked me what was wrong. The words "my aunt has HIV" tumbled out of my mouth.

We sat on the grass and just talked for hours. Mainly, I talked and cried, and he listened and made jokes to make me laugh. I told him about my aunt, how much I loved her and how she was the sanest, coolest person in my family. She was the family rebel, the adventurous one—always doing something new and cool—and she was always honest with me. I loved her most for that. Stories and emotions poured out of me endlessly and Nick just smiled and took them in.

We didn't move from our spot on the grass until curfew, when he walked me to the furthest spot that boys could venture before entering the girls' dorm area, gave me another hug, and told me, "It'll be ok." It was Nick, so I believed him. Then I headed into my dorm room, washed up, and went to sleep. The next day, I called the program director to tell her my grandmother wouldn't be able to give me the other half of the trip fee after all. I didn't go into details and just thanked her for trying to help me. She said it was fine and then I ended the call, feeling guilty that I'd even wanted to go on the trip in the first place.

I carried that guilt secretly through my senior year of high school when, in a moment of frustration, my aunt shared that she was tired of her mother—my grandmother—asking her for money. Confused by the comment, I asked what she meant. It turned out my aunt had been giving my grandmother money for years—bailing her out whenever she called and asked for help. My grandmother had never given my aunt a dime to help my aunt with her medical care and, in fact, had treated my aunt pretty badly all her life. As my aunt vented about her mother only calling her when she needed something, about years of broken promises and withheld love, I stayed quiet.

I didn't bother telling my aunt about the study abroad trip and what my grandmother did. I just listened while my brain tried to process the truth. My grandmother lied to me and was never planning to give me money for that trip. She only told me she would so I would feel dependent on her. Then she used my aunt's HIV diagnosis to guilt me, so I'd never question her. She was never trying to help me; she was just laying the groundwork to be able to use me in the future. I never shared this with my aunt or even my mother. I had witnessed the dysfunctional hold that my grandmother had on them and knew telling them would just be considered stirring up trouble. So I kept it to myself, but I promised myself that I wouldn't give my grandmother the power to crush my hopes again.

I didn't have to wait too long to test my resolve. During my sophomore year of college, I did what everyone tells students not to do: I applied for a credit card. I figured I could use it to buy my textbooks at the beginning of each semester and pay it off throughout the year, since I was usually strapped after paying the balance of my tuition that my scholarship and student loans did not cover. I had been working since I was fourteen and paid all my bills on time, so I figured I'd be approved with a credit limit high enough to cover my book costs. Color me shocked when the credit card rep told me I was declined for a card.

One of the three jobs I worked in college was at a retail store that had its own store credit card that I had to try to get people to sign up for, so I knew the drill of what people needed to do when they were declined. I had to wait until the next morning, but I got up early to call the credit bureau, Equifax. I assumed there was a simple mistake somewhere on my account since I never had a credit card before, and that I could get it fixed by calling. After an exceedingly long hold, I got through to a representative who let me know this was not a simple mistake but that there were three open credit cards with large past due balances linked to my name and social security number. Upset at learning that my identity had been stolen, I asked what address they had on file for the fraudulent credit cards. She told me the address and I recognized it immediately: it was my grandmother's.

Now very, very pissed off, I tried telling the credit bureau representative that they were fraudulent cards, but she said I'd have to work with the credit card companies directly to get them closed and removed from my credit report. She gave me the phone numbers for each of the credit card companies and told me to give them a call.

After we hung up, I dialed my mother immediately and told her what my grandmother had done. I was heated and told her how awful this was and how having bad credit could jeopardize my scholarship. I let her know that if I had to file a police report, I would give them my grandmother's name and address and she would just have to deal with it. My mom was apologetic on the phone but said there was nothing she could do to help, which made me more frustrated. She'd tried to be really supportive of me ever since we were reunified, but her mother was always a blind spot. And this moment was no different. I just told her I needed to start calling the credit card companies to get this fixed.

The first company I called told me they couldn't list the card as fraudulent and close it because it had been open for five years with partial payments made every month. I would need to prove I wasn't the one who opened the card. When I said, "Five years means that the credit card had been open when I was 15 years old and not legal because I was a minor," the representative quickly changed their tune and said, "I've closed that card and listed it as fraud."

The other two credit cards were more difficult to get flagged as fraud because they had been opened after I turned eighteen, and payments had been made sporadically on each of the cards. Also, because the credit bureaus had my grandmother's address listed as mine for more than five years, it was now linked to my credit report as verified information. It was a mess, and I was on the phone for two hours collecting all the information I needed for the police report they told me I would need to file to get the fraudulent claims started.

As I hung up the phone, I saw my grandmother's number light up on my screen. For a second, I stared at it, debating what to do. And then I decided to deal with it head-on. Before I could get a word out, my grandmother laid into me: "You selfish beast" was the first thing I heard. Then came, "I wouldn't have gotten those cards if I didn't need them." "After everything I did for you, taking you in." "You would have been on the f******* streets." "You have no right to close the cards." "You're so ungrateful."

My face got hot, and the nastiest retorts formed in my brain. I was about to go off when it hit me. I'd heard her curse people out like this before. Usually, it was my mom or my aunt after they made some perceived slight against her. She'd go all in on them, call them every name but a child of God, and tell them how they, not her, were the problem. She'd then guilt them about being an "ungrateful" daughter and proceed to cut off communication with them until they'd crack days, weeks, or months later and give her a call. I'd watched her do this for years. As I held the phone away from my ear—because she was yelling so loud—I thought to myself, *I am not one of your daughters.* I said the word "nope" to myself and hung up the phone. She dialed me back, but I didn't pick up.

I called my mom instead to let her know I was done dealing with my grandmother and that I didn't want to hear any updates from her or about her ever again. I did this to preempt any guilt trips that my grandmother might or would try to lay on my mom to pressure me to apologize. It took me a full year of going back and forth via phone and snail mail with the credit card companies and credit bureaus to get the fraudulent credit cards and negative marks on my credit reports removed. But I did it.

By the time my senior year rolled around, I had gone more than a year without engaging with my grandmother and all I felt was peace. Every once in a while, my mom or aunt would mention something about her—she called for money, she wasn't speaking with one of them for one reason or another. But when she would come up in conversation, I would keep quiet and not respond, and the topic would change. I was done with that cycle of abuse and refused to let it be passed down to another generation.

Halfway through the first semester of my last year of college, I came across a study abroad flyer promoting my school's program in London. The trauma of my failed Russian trip flooded my mind, and I started to just walk past the flyer, but something in me made me freeze.

I'd made so much happen for myself, why shouldn't I see if I could figure this out too? I noted the contact details and went straight to my dorm to email and find out the details for the program. It turned out my scholarship could be applied to the educational components of the program, but the application deadline was in three days. I raced to get letters of referral from my professors, complete all the paperwork, and submit everything on time. I got in.

It turned out that room, board, and flights were not covered by my scholarship, but they would be comped if I applied and was accepted to be a resident advisor for the program. I did and was accepted to that too. The only problem I had was I didn't see how I could make enough money to support myself for six months outside of the country. Nearly all the money I made went to cover my school and food costs already. Hesitation crept into my mind, but I figured that since all the stars had aligned already—with me beating the program submission date, getting accepted, and not having to pay for a flight or a place to stay—I would make the lack of funds work out too… somehow.

About two weeks after I arrived in London, my college emailed me to let me know that since the study abroad program actually cost less than my scholarship and loans combined, they would be refunding me the balance of funds. It was around $4,000. Hitting the lottery wouldn't have made me as happy as that email did. It took two months for the school to refund me, so I made a habit of showing up to all the program's free catered meal events, bought cheap groceries, and used my new credit card when I was tapped. It also turned out that unlike in the US, the RAs in the study abroad program got paid $500. It was a double help, especially since there was an error between the London campus team and the US team, and all the RAs got paid twice. None of the other RAs brought up the second payment windfall, and I wasn't about to either.

Money was tight the entire time I was studying abroad—doubly so because my mom had fallen down a flight of stairs and broken her leg back home, so I was sending her money to help cover some bills—but that did not stop me from having one of the most incredible experiences of my life. The program really pushed us students to immerse ourselves in the culture and offered tons of opportunities to engage. I signed up for every free museum, theater, and city tour they offered. I saw musicals on the West End and opera at the Royal Opera House, and I ate my way through Borough Market. I walked and took the bus everywhere I could so I could take it all in, and I had all the streets and parks near my flat memorized. The neatly woven houses in South Kensington—where the program's flats were located—reminded me a lot of Striver's Row, one of the richest blocks in Harlem, and that made me feel not too far from home.

I liked London and it turned out I liked traveling, too. With my scrappy financial creativity, I was able to swing side trips to cities in Spain, Morocco, and of course, France. Paris was every bit as spectacular as *Funny Face* made it out to be. I actually ended up visiting the city twice during my time in the program and fell in love with the vibe, nightlife, food, and fashion. Taking that leap of faith and applying for the London program literally expanded my world, and it was the reminder I needed that I was capable of doing big things on my own.

The study abroad program ended about a week before my graduation, so I flew back to the States with a whirlwind list of items to take care of in preparation for receiving my diploma. My mom, who had moved to Jersey City while I was in college, decided to relocate to Florida while I was in London. She found me an apartment a few doors down from her old place in Jersey City. I used the last of my London money to pay the security deposit and first month's rent and moved into a completely empty apartment, save for my old twin bed. Finding a job quickly was high on my list but I wanted to get through graduation first. In the midst of confirming where I could pick up my cap and gown when I headed back to Boston, a call beeped on the other line of my cell phone. Since I was on hold, I switched over without looking at the screen and said hello.

"I was surprised to not receive an invite for your graduation," said my grandmother. I hadn't spoken to her in more than two years at this point, and it took a second for her voice to register in my mind. Before I could respond, she continued, "You would have been on the street if it wasn't for me." She started to say something else, but I'll never know what it was because I hung up on her and went back to holding on the other line for my cap and gown pickup details. After I got all the information I needed, I calmly left my apartment, hopped on the PATH train and then the subway, and walked into a cellphone store. I walked out with a new phone and a new phone number. My first call was to my mom to make sure she had my number and to tell her not to share it with my grandmother, *ever*. No longer was I willing to try to keep the peace with unpeaceful people.

I had found my own peace, and I was willing to do whatever it took to protect it. To break free from the cycle of guilt, manipulation, and chaos—even from family—I had to let go. Choosing my well-being over others wasn't selfish, it wasn't survival, it was growth. It was a recognition that I deserved a life free from others' baggage, filled with genuine joy and contentment. The path to peace may not always be easy, but it's always worth it. You have the power to choose it for yourself, and once you do, you'll realize you've created space for the wonder that life has to offer.

PART II
Adapting & Healing

CHAPTER 9
Quitting Is an Act of Self Care

THERE HAVE BEEN several instances in my life where toughing out a difficult situation has enriched my life for the better. There was the time during a kinship-care placement—where youth in foster care are placed with family or friends—when my "stepsister" did my hair in tight curly coils. I actually have no idea if she and I were legal "stepsiblings" because the adults in my life have always been a little fuzzy on the technicalities. But she was older than me and in charge of doing my hair while I lived with her family.

After she removed my headscarf and rollers, tears spilled down my plump face as I stared in the mirror and saw the scrunched style on my grade school head that adults unkindly shared was too big for my age. I begged her to put my hair in a ponytail instead of making me wear it this way, but she refused. The next day during morning attendance, I tried to melt into my chair as I squeaked "present" when my teacher called my name. She scanned me quickly and without missing a beat, said, "I like your hair today," before calling out the next name on the list. I beamed brightly for the rest of the day and gleefully asked for my stepsister to do my hair the same way the following week.

Plenty of doors opened to me because I went to an elite private boarding school—and doing so taught me how to navigate rooms that I wasn't expected to be in. Boarding school became the linchpin for the narrative I'd recount to allay concerns that I saw in the dismissive eyes of future employers. You'll never quite know the power of privilege until you watch a gatekeeper's face's muscles soften as you answer their question, "Tell me about yourself," with, "I'm a native New Yorker who grew up in the heart of Manhattan. I attended a college prep boarding school where I learned to ride horseback western style and was a top-ranked tennis champ there before attending college in Boston." I wielded those strategically selected facts to lockpick myself into rooms for much of my early career—and stopped only when I was confident my professional experience and reputation spoke for themselves.

It was in one of those rooms—one that I'd worked hard to talk my way into—that I learned one of my first big lessons of the professional world. It was my first office job post-college. I was in the ladies' room and had just turned the water on to wash my hands when a vice president walked out from a stall and said to me, "HR told me you listed your salary on your form as $32,000."

Confused, I responded, "Yes. That's what I was told the salary was for this job."

"It is *up to* $32,000," she snapped back. I didn't reply, so we awkwardly stood there in the bathroom and stared at each other for 20 seconds (but going on eternity). Finally, I shrugged my shoulders and said, "Well, I was told it was $32,000." She washed her hands and left the ladies' room. A whole *three hours* into the first day of my new job, alarm bells were going off in my head.

Things continued on a steadily negative pace from there. During my team welcome lunch at a restaurant close to the office a few days later, that same VP was aghast when I ordered meatloaf and mashed potatoes for lunch while the rest of the team ordered sandwiches. Honestly, it was my first corporate lunch, and I didn't know there was an unspoken expectation in the business world that everyone was supposed to order something "light" for lunch like a soup, salad, or sandwich. I didn't understand what the big deal was since I really enjoyed meatloaf and mashed potatoes, and my meal was about the same price as the lunches my team members had ordered. I sat there stone-faced and hot, trying not to cry from embarrassment, while the VP made not one, not two, but three separate jokes about my order.

I'd ignored the warning bells again a few months later when, during a late-night deadline that by now had become a regular occurrence, a female co-worker jokingly let me in on the office pastime of trying to look down my dress to guess my breast size. Apparently, the fact that the tiniest sliver of my cleavage showed in the neckline of my dresses was a game-worthy distraction for men much senior to me in both title and age. Instead of exiting stage right, I chose to start layering button-up blouses under my dresses from that point forward. It would be a couple of weeks later—dressed in my new chic puritan look—where'd I make a mistake of detrimental proportion.

During a team-building exercise where I must have eaten too many catered cookies and been on a sugar high, I mindlessly dropped my armor and answered a question without thinking. The question: "Tell us one thing about yourself that no one here knows." It was an exercise based on speed, so we blurted out responses in the order we sat around the conference room table. My colleagues gave professionally acceptable responses of their favorite foods, quirky pet names, and childhood fears of things like clowns, and they were each rewarded with a kind group laugh or warm comment of "how cute" or "love it." Instead of following suit with a throwaway fact, I gave the truthful answer of, "I was in foster care as a child."

Without missing a beat, my boss chimed in, "I didn't know that about *you*." I'll never forget the seriousness and look of horror on her face as she said those words, and I knew there was no fixing my unforced error. Over the weeks that followed, I found myself dreading going to work and counting the hours until the day was done. Before my admission, I was a stellar employee who received public office recognition for my work efforts and accomplishments; now, my every move required scrutiny and oversight by my boss. Routine trainings—that I had led alone since the second week I was hired—suddenly required a debriefing session with my boss so I could keep her apprised. Confusingly, expense reports I submitted were suddenly rejected for having too many single subway fares on them for training sessions—we rode the subways to and from training locations—because I was spending too much on travel. To save money, I started purchasing unlimited weekly subway cards, but those expense reports were rejected as well, because they could potentially be used by me for a personal subway ride. Each encounter with her became a damned if I do, damned if I don't situation.

Each day brought a new moment of deflation that wore on me. The worst moment was after I'd secured a big-name celebrity to speak to some of the youth in our program. Even early in my career, I knew it was an amazing feat, and I had done it all on my own. I called the celebrity's office repeatedly, and after months of efforts, I convinced their team to host a group of twenty of our youth for an hour talk and Q&A session with the A-lister. It was such a big deal that the PR firm representing our organization secured media to attend the talk with our students and the celebrity. That made me extra excited because I hadn't been able to find a job in public relations when I graduated college, so my plan was to take any opportunity I could find and try to use it to help me get into PR in the future.

Getting to spend an afternoon with the PR agency and letting them see what I was capable of was exactly the type of opportunity I wanted to create for myself. And knowing that I was able to create this awesome experience for some of the organization's youth to meet a celebrity they admired made the moment even more fulfilling.

On the day of the actual event, the excitement and smiles on the faces were so bright they have stayed with me to this day. Each of them got to pose a question to the celeb, and each received a heartfelt answer. Our host was gracious, humble, and with his encouraging words he challenged the kids to defy the limitations that had been set for them. The pride on the faces of these teens as they walked out of that room and into the sun-filled day was undeniable.

In addition to doing all the interviews the PR agency set up, the celebrity promised to send me copies of his book to give to all the students—which made all the students even more excited when he told them. True to his word, the books arrived about a week later. It was the end of the school year, so the easiest way to get the copies to the students was to mail them to their individual homes. I had already had the students write down their addresses for me before I dismissed them on event day. So, as I sat at my desk stuffing books into padded envelopes and affixing address labels to them, I was feeling pretty proud of myself for pulling the entire event together. I didn't even hear my boss walk up behind me.

"What are these?" she said as she picked up one of the books.

"They're books for the students who attended the event last week. I'm mailing them their copies."

"Oh, okay," she said as she turned to walk away with the book still in her hand.

"Um, I need that book," I quickly called out. "I only requested enough books for the students to have a copy."

She turned back to me and again said, "Oh, okay," but kept the book in her hand. I hadn't had the foresight to request more books than I needed for the students who attended the event, and as she stood clutching one in hand, I realized that this oversight was going to be an issue.

Still holding the book tightly in her hand, she said, "You didn't request approval to ship out items, and we don't have the budget for this. I'm going to update Tim," another VP at our company, "on this." I knew as she said this that my shipping books to students really shouldn't have been a problem—we actually sent items like awards to students often, and I was shipping the books as media mail, the cheapest way you can mail something in the US. I was also under budget for the event since the celebrity's office had covered snacks for the students. Her problem wasn't that books were being shipped to the students; her problem was that *I* was shipping books to students. Even in that moment I knew that her problem was illogically *with me* and nothing I could do or say would make a difference.

So, I just said, "Okay," as she turned and made a beeline for the VP's office. I kept stuffing books into the manila-colored envelopes and attaching labels, biting my lower lip but staying focused on the task. I actually had gotten budget approval to mail out the books days before from the very VP she headed off to update, but I knew it would benefit me in no way to share that information with her. A few minutes later, she returned to my cubicle, placed the book on my desk, and said, "This is fine," before walking towards her office—with a little pep missing from her step. I had won the battle, and it felt surprisingly good, but later, as the events replayed in my mind, I realized that I hadn't signed up for this war.

A couple of weeks later, while she was chastising me in her office for something trivial—I honestly don't remember what exactly—I heard myself say aloud, "Why don't we make today my last day here." It was early in the day on a Monday, but I was just exhausted: tired of being belittled, tired of having to fight to do my job, and more than anything, tired of her treating me like I was untrustworthy because I had been in foster care. As soon as I uttered those words, I actually felt the weight of all that exhaustion lift from my body. I was overwhelmed with instantaneous relief. My—now former—manager went silent and turned a little red. She would go on to spend the next 20 minutes trying to talk me out of my decision to quit, even asking me, "Why do you feel we can't find a solution?"

I wanted to bust out laughing when she said that. I had found a solution—I just quit! It just turned out it wasn't a solution she had considered me taking. When she couldn't convince me to "go home and sleep on it," she shifted to trying to get me to agree to stay for two weeks to pass on my work to other team members. I paused to think about it and immediately felt anxiety building within me. So, I calmly told her that didn't work for me. Before she could respond, I started rattling off details about my major open projects and letting her know where she could find documents on the team server. She stared at me for about a minute but then turned her chair and began typing notes into her laptop. I wrapped up my brain dump of information and let her know I was going to talk to finance about my final paycheck and then leave.

With that, I stood up and walked out of her office and popped into the finance manager's office to chat. This conversation was quick and cordial. I told him I was quitting, and he let me know when I'd receive my final paycheck, including my vacation pay. I said goodbye, walked over to my desk, grabbed my phone and my purse, and left. I felt so good and had zero regrets. Until the next day.

After falling asleep blissfully calm, I woke up still resolved but worried. I only had a few hundred dollars saved and it wasn't enough to cover my half of the rent for the apartment I was sharing with my friend. I hadn't been actively searching for a job, so I didn't have so much as an interview lined up. It was Tuesday, so I couldn't even hang out and commiserate—or celebrate—with my friends, since they were all at work. Doubt ran wild through my head. I started to wonder if I shouldn't have quit, but as soon as I had that thought—all my anxiety disappeared. Just the thought of putting myself back in the position to be undermined and disrespected again made my worries about the future seem trivial. I had no idea what tomorrow held, but I knew my terrible boss and going to a job she made toxic weren't part of it. Fretting about the future seemed frivolous since it already felt brighter.

I happily laughed at that thought, sauntered out of bed, made myself some breakfast, and promptly logged online to look for a new job. Fortunately, I found a temp job that I was able to start a few days later that covered my half of the rent and my living expenses. Less than two months later, with the help of an old friend, I landed a new full-time role doing data entry for a fashion company that paid me more than the job I quit. Reflecting back on it all, my sole regret is hesitating to quit for as long as I did. Lingering in an environment that I knew was having a detrimental impact on my mental health was unwise. I'd spent so long trying to talk my way into those rooms I wasn't supposed to be in, it hadn't occurred to me that there were a good number of them I didn't even *want* to be in.

Quitting isn't always the answer in life, but it shouldn't be stigmatized as the answer of last resort either. If something isn't good for you—a food, a habit, a person, an environment, a job—you should never be made to feel ashamed for walking away from it. Rather, quitting is an act of self-care, a testament to valuing one's well-being, and to asserting the right to exist on terms that serve you. Once I got comfortable with that, it was hard to limit myself to anything less.

CHAPTER 10
Bet on You

MY FIRST TRIP to Las Vegas was for work. I had been on a few business trips before but never to a place that conjured up so much angst in my mind as "Sin City." The only reference points for my opinion of Vegas were movies I had seen over the years: in Stephen King's *The Stand,* it's the place where good *literally* has its final confrontation with evil; in *Leaving Las Vegas,* it's the place where a person who gave up on life *literally* drinks themselves to death; and in the original *Ocean's Eleven,* it's where a group of thieves execute the crime of a lifetime but still lose everything in a not-too-subtle metaphor—the house always wins in the end. If you haven't seen those movies, sorry about the spoilers.

Nevertheless, this was the location of the most important job I had been tasked with in my short but budding career, and I was excited. I even purchased my first ever carry-on luggage for the trip, a rolling bag in a bright pink shade that made me smile. I was doing a national campaign shoot with a living musical legend, and I wasn't about to screw it up. There was a lot riding on this shoot and I had moved heaven and earth to make it happen, including flying in our preferred photographer, securing a studio last minute, tracking down a rider-approved chef to cook with grapeseed oil, and successfully convincing the talent's management team that the locally secured bottled water would be just as thirst-quenching as their rider-required bottle that would've needed to be flown in from France. There were a few hiccups in the day—like the diva artist showing up four hours late for the shoot—but I beamed with too much pride from all I'd accomplished to let that put a damper on my mood. It took a lot to get me here and I was going to enjoy every moment.

Let's rewind a few months. I was a 23-year-old who had weathered my first recession by the seat of my pants and had managed to parlay an entry-level data entry role (I literally transcribed the names, addresses, and emails from customer cards into a database) into a Public Relations and Marketing Manager position in less than a year. Even all these years later, I'm still impressed with myself for pulling that off.

From the start, I knew that I didn't want the data entry job at all. But I wanted to work in fashion public relations. And this role was with a bona fide fashion company that was hiring and interested in me. A friend of mine worked there and had recommended me for the role. I wasn't deterred by the fact that they didn't even have a public relations department. They had a marketing department, which is the department the data entry role fell under. So, I figured that if I took the job, there might be an opportunity for me to eventually move to a more central marketing role and maybe even do some public relations tasks as part of it.

So, I took the data entry role—and pretended to really want the job. And I mean really pretended because I disliked every single moment of it.

But honestly, it wasn't a bad job. It was just mind-numbingly tedious. During purchases, store associates would attempt to collect personal information from customers and enter it into the register, if they had time. If not, they would have the customer fill out their information on a customer card and the associate would mail it to corporate to be entered by someone else. That someone was me.

My sad, small cubicle was stacked with at least two dozen baskets—the ones the postal service carries letters in—filled with thousands of customer cards. There were stacks of customer cards on the floor, under my desk, on my desk, on my chair, in my filing cabinet. They were everywhere. I spent my first day at work rearranging the stacks so I could enter my cubicle without them falling on top of me and clearing my desk so I could set up my computer to enter the information on the cards.

The database program would assign each entry a customer number so the company could track the purchase habits of customers. The goal was to see what clothing or accessories were purchased together to arm the Fashion Merchant Team—the "buyers"—with data they could use to better inform their orders. Of all the departments at the fashion company, the buyers were clearly the most important and most influential team. They made all the decisions on what styles were purchased for the stores, managed the relationships with all the fashion vendors, and set the tone for the entire retail chain.

Unfortunately, we never had good enough data from the system to positively impact sales. And even worse, I was the one that had to share the unhelpful reports in the weekly merchandising meeting with all the buyers and heads of the departments and one board member who was also a large investor in the company. My presentations during the meetings usually ended with the investor/board member stating, "That's not enough information to do anything with," which of course I had no retort for since he was completely correct.

After months of doing these embarrassingly unhelpful report presentations at the merchandising meetings and shrinking whenever the investor/board member would slam the result, I had the bright idea to suggest some ways to actually make the system more effective and help gather better data. I wanted to show them that I was invested in helping the merchandising team and the company, so I spent time chatting with the database company and researching customer data collection methods online, and I put together a few ideas to make it better. At the end of my weekly report, I boldly and confidently made the statement, "We can get better results if we capture more data regularly." I was ready to follow that up with a few suggestions that I had written out in my note from the research I gathered. But before I could utter out another word, the investor/board member shot back with, "That's why we have you!"

Shocked at the sharp shutdown and quick shift of energy in the room, all I was able to stammer out was a single "Oh, ok" before silently slinking back into my seat. The room moved onto the next agenda item, and the conversation shifted. Once the meeting was over, I collected my notes and, majorly dumbfounded, headed back to my desk to try and figure out how I had managed to screw up that opportunity to show everyone I knew what I was talking about.

Didn't they want me to figure out ways to get the database to give us better information that we could use to make better merchandise-buying decisions? That would save the company tons of money in the long run. Didn't they want me to learn all I could about the system and report what I learned to them? I mean, wasn't that why they included me in the merchandising meeting every week? Why was I presenting if what I was presenting wasn't helpful? I mean, why did they hire me if not to do this job as well as I could?

I was pretty confused but determined to figure out what I did wrong. Over the next few weeks, I made changes to help me find out the answer. Instead of coming in and heading straight to my grey cave to get my work done, I started frequenting the morning breakfast truck that would park outside our office building around 9 a.m. each morning. This gave me time to interact with my co-workers for a few minutes before starting the day, and I discovered that I didn't know anyone particularly well, especially the people in the marketing department.

So, I also started hanging out in their area of my floor more so I could get to know everyone better. I'd pop over there in the morning to eat my breakfast I bought from the food truck—cereal and a piece of fruit, or a bacon, egg, and cheese sandwich when I could splurge. I'd ask about their weekends, boyfriends, wives, and kids. We'd talk about what they were working on or prepping to work on. The marketing team was filled with some cool creatives, and they did everything from retouching photoshoot images to designing store signs, banners, and billboards.

After a few weeks, I got into a good rapport with just about everyone on the team, and pretty soon they started inviting me to lunch and even popping by my cubicle throughout the day to chitchat. As I became closer to the team, my mood also began to shift about my job. I began looking forward to coming to the office each day, and my cubicle didn't feel nearly as dreary.

As my co-workers and I became closer, they shared details on how the office really worked. They shared the fact that everyone—especially the investor/board member—vehemently disliked my boss. Apparently, she had a very impressive resume but had failed to do anything of substance in the year she had been working for the company. I already had strong reservations about my boss before they shared this information with me. This was the woman who onboarded me to my new role by dropping off the database manual and the phone number to the company's customer service line and telling me to call it with any questions I had because she didn't have the time to deal with database questions. In my time there, I had only chatted with her a handful of times, and she seldom checked in on me to find out how any of my work was progressing.

She was also never really around. I hadn't thought much of her coming in late and leaving early until senior people—including HR—started stopping by my cubicle to ask me if I had seen her or knew where she was. During lunch with my new work friends, I mentioned the fact that people were constantly asking me where our boss was and being confused about why they were asking me.

"It's because you're her hire," was the response they shared.

Apparently, my boss had pushed the executive team into buying the database system by saying that her previous company used it and it worked really well. The purchase ate up a big part of the marketing budget but hadn't helped the merchandising team improve sales at all. The executive team was frustrated and there were rumors that they wanted to let her go. She had convinced them that hiring a data entry person would help. But she couldn't get approval to hire a data entry person with experience, so she went with a cheaper option—hiring me. As my co-workers talked, it became very clear to me that I was nothing but a pawn to my boss and expendable to the executive team.

Later, when I was back in my cubicle, I started planning. My boss wasn't going to be around for the long haul, and if I wanted to not be fired with her, then I needed to change people from thinking I was "her hire." I needed to show them that I was part of the wider team.

It's strange that we put so much stock in college being the place to prepare you for the working world when it's the rules of the high school cafeteria that determine so much of business success. I needed to be smart, strategic, and diplomatic—yes! But essentially, I needed to get invited to the popular kids' table. So, I got to work to try and make that happen.

The friend of mine who had recommended me for the job worked as the assistant to the company's Head of Merchandising (HOM). Her boss was one of the most important women in the organization, and she had wide influence over the day-to-day decisions that happened within those fashion walls. On paper, my boss didn't report into Merchandising, but in reality, no fashion creative she oversaw made its way out into the world without the HOM's approval.

The lines between Marketing and Merchandising were also blurred when it came to experiential activations like store openings. The company was in the midst of a massive expansion, opening hundreds of stores across the country. Creative was responsible for creating all the signage within the store. But it was the merchandising team that HOM oversaw that was responsible for promoting the store opening within the local community. The goal with every store was to make it feel like an integral part of the community so that women felt excited to shop there.

Opening day for a new store usually included an in-store fashion show, a DJ, and some gift-card giveaways to customers. The HOM assigned her assistant, my friend, to oversee the planning of opening days—rather than the Marketing team. Looking back, I don't think there was any spiteful intent underpinning this decision. Honestly, I think she just wanted someone who she trusted and would give her regular updates to be in charge of store opening day promotions. In the grand scheme of her world—managing about a two dozen buyers and visual merchandisers, overseeing millions of dollars of inventory, minimizing losses, keeping tabs on and approving store creative, and keeping the board updated—assigning someone to hire a DJ, find some models to wear some clothes, and hand out gift cards probably wasn't a worry that was keeping her up at night.

Regardless, I saw an opportunity and committed to shooting my shot.

After the next merchandising meeting, I lingered around to help "tidy up" the conference room. I knew my boss would book it out of the meeting as soon as it was over while the HOM would stay behind to chat with the board member who always attended. All I needed was for her to say anything at all to me—anything at all—and I was ready. She just needed to give me an opening, and I was ready to walk through it. It took what felt like an eternity of me intently picking up left-behind agendas and pushing in rolling chairs for her to wrap up her conversation and acknowledge me, but she did.

"That meeting went well. How are you today?"

"I'm really good. How are you?"

"I'm doing well, just busy."

"Yeah, I totally understand." I didn't, but it felt like the right response.

I continued, "Um, I know there's another store opening next weekend. If you want, I could write a media alert to try to get local reporters to attend the event. I've written them before." That was true. I'd done them in college. For homework. I tried to keep cool.

"I don't know what that is."

"Oh, a media alert is an informational one-sheet with all the key event details for reporters, so they can decide if they want to attend or cover the event. It might help us get more people out to the store."

"We've never done one before. If you think it would help, write one and I'll look over it."

"Ok. I'll get that to you tomorrow."

That was it. But it's always the moments that seem small that have the power to change everything.

I went back to my desk and got to work writing the media alert with what was left of the workday, ignoring the customer cards piled in my cubicle that afternoon. I felt a ton of anxiety but wanted to blow the HOM away. I knew this could be my opportunity to really impress her, and I wanted to do just that. Not only did I need that media alert to be great—well written, error-free, and engaging enough for reporters to be intrigued and cover our store opening—but I also wanted it to show her that I was smart and, by extension, valuable. I needed three hundred words on a single page to do a heck of a lot. It was my one shot.

I printed out the draft and worked on it more on the train ride home. Then I worked on it late into the evening. I didn't have a laptop at the time because I couldn't afford one, so I wrote all my changes on the printout and then rewrote the entire thing by hand in a notebook. I got to work an hour earlier the next morning to retype the media alert and made sure it was as tight as possible. I read it aloud like 10 times to make sure every word, syllable, and comma was right.

Then I printed out a clean copy and brought it over to the HOM to review. It was still early in the morning, so the office was just starting to come to life. Her assistant wasn't at her desk, so I popped my head in and said, "Good morning," and handed it to her to read. She read it then and there and told me I could send it out—just like that. So, I went back to my still-customer-card-stacked hidey-hole of a cubicle to track down the email and phone numbers of reporters in the city where the store was opening. I built a media list of around fifty reporters and spent the next week emailing them the media alert and leaving them voice messages, kindly (and maybe a little desperately) inviting them to attend. I made getting press to that store opening my mission and worked on nothing else that week. Luckily, my boss was MIA as usual, so she was none the wiser that I had shifted my focus and was letting the customer cards pile up as I went hard on pitching.

I'd love to say that all my efforts led to a slew of reporters attending and that we were overrun with positive press coverage, but in the end, I only enticed one lone local newspaper reporter to attend the event. One single reporter felt my media alert—and consistent but probably irksome voicemail reminders—to have been compelling enough to warrant writing a single story to appear in the local paper.

But sometimes one is enough.

It turned out that the lone newspaper story was the first one the brand had gotten on a store opening, and it was a super positive article. The HOM was excited when I shared it with her, and she turned around and shared it with our CEO—letting him know "Charell" had secured it. The CEO shared it with the entire company board, who were ecstatic to have the brand highlighted in the news. The investor/ board member who had called me out a few weeks prior congratulated me on my hard work the next time I saw him. And, with that, I had shed the label of being my boss's "hire" and became a vital member of the team.

Over the next few weeks, I became more involved with the store openings, and it became the expectation that I would reach out to media in each city to try to generate more positive coverage for the brand. No one officially verbalized the shift in my job responsibilities, but they did ask me for press updates during the merchandising meetings. So, it was clear that I was no longer being judged solely on the success of the database. A few weeks later, my boss was out. She had a public war of words with that investor/board member and was unceremoniously fired the next day.

The HOM's assistant was put in charge of the marketing department, and I became the HOM's new assistant—gladly leaving the customer database and my grey cubicle behind. I still assisted with the store openings, and my responsibilities expanded to a mix of public relations and marketing duties that included helping produce the campaign photoshoots, writing speeches for my new boss, and getting our fashion collections featured in magazines. After a couple of months of rocking my role, I was officially promoted to Public Relations and Marketing Manager and was given a desk in the even brighter marketing area.

Fast-forward a few months, and I found myself in Las Vegas, actually carving out my own professional path. Sometimes in life, all you can do is play the hand you're dealt. Much of my life in foster care was just that—a game of high stakes with a few wild cards thrown in. But not everything in life can be left to chance. When you see an opportunity to show the world what you can do, you should seize it with the confidence of a seasoned gambler going all in on a royal flush. After all, fortune favors the bold, and I was determined to bet on myself and turn the odds in my favor, one daring step at a time.

CHAPTER 11
Off Route Doesn't Mean Off Track

HERE'S A WELL-EARNED lesson: if a company you've never heard of contacts you out of the blue with an amazing job opportunity and makes you an offer after one round of interviews, run!

Looking back, there were so many warning signs.

Looking back, I should have seen the red flags.

I was too green in my professional career and too flattered by the fact that an actual New York City public relations agency wanted to poach me to recognize them. Besides the short interview process and quick offer (red flag #1), there was a hard-pressure push from their Human Resources vice president to get me to start in two weeks. I had wanted to give my fashion company three weeks' notice, not because I had to, but because I generally liked the people I worked with and wanted to make sure I transitioned everything over to my colleagues and gave them time to ask me questions. When I emailed my start date to the new company, I received an immediate call on my cell, telling me I didn't "owe my current company anything" and that they really needed me to start in two weeks. They didn't threaten to rescind the offer, but they made it sound like I'd be starting off on the wrong foot if I didn't start within the two weeks: red flag #2.

Once I joined, they walked me around the office and introduced me to everyone, which was nice. There was a welcome lunch for me that first day as well. But the onboarding process consisted of them showing me how to access the team drive and telling me to read the materials in the client folder—press releases, product fact sheets, and executive bios. There was no rundown of their client's goals or review of the work the agency had done in the past. I spent my first two days just opening documents, reading them, and trying to learn as much about the brand as I could on my own: red flag #3. And, on my third day, they told me we would be meeting with the client the following day and I would be helping them present a big campaign idea to them: red flag #4.

I spent all day reviewing the presentation deck and huddling with the presenting team, which consisted of two male vice presidents, one White and one Hispanic, and one Black female consultant. It hadn't escaped my notice during my office tour that there was a lack of diversity on the team. I only met one Hispanic employee (the VP) and one other Black employee (the consultant) in their New York office of about sixty people. Both had started at the firm just a few short weeks prior to me and both were part of the client presentation: red flag #5.

It was my first agency presentation, so I was pretty nervous, but the clients were very friendly, and I had all but memorized my slides and speaking parts. It also helped my nerves that I was actually very familiar with the clients' brand. Our client was one of the largest spirits producers and distributors in the world. After I graduated college, I had actually worked nights and weekends as a promo girl for an experiential staffing company, offering free samples of various spirits to customers at off-premise locations like liquor and wine shops and also on-premise ones like clubs and bars. The staffing company held detailed multi-hour trainings on all the liquors and audience targets we sampled, so I was pretty knowledgeable about the products, even if my PR agency had done a lackluster job of educating me on the overall goals of the brand.

The big idea we were trying to sell was a barbershop-based event series targeting African American men to help promote one of the client's large liquor brands. The concept wasn't an original one—dozens of lifestyle brands have done similar activations targeting the same audience—but it was a new and pretty safe idea for this client, and they were generally excited by the proposal. Their only hesitation was that they felt we needed a stronger hook to get the media and press to attend and cover the events, which was our job as an agency after all: red flag #6. The White VP on our team said we would look into some celebrity talent and get back to them with some ideas. The client said that was fine but asked if we had any off-the-top "relevant" recommendations we could share now.

The loudness of the silence was deafening and as I watched the VP stammer, it dawned on me that he didn't know a single appropriate celebrity talent to recommend that would be relevant to a Black audience: red flag #7. He blurted out something about needing to check the Q-scores of some talent before making a recommendation, at which moment I could see frowns creep across the faces of our clients. Q-scores, I would come to learn, are a marketing tool for scoring the popularity of brands, entertainment products like movies, and celebrities. They can be totally helpful in ensuring a talent will appeal to your audience, but the VP's suggestion of them sounded like a less than reassuring crutch to our clients, who were looking for an impromptu confirmation that we—the agency they paid to build awareness for their brands—really knew their audience.

Unprompted, and totally off script, I chimed in with a few talent names that I thought could work for the campaign activation. One was an up-and-coming singer who was becoming really well-known in the Black community. I had a good rapport with her manager from my time working in fashion and suggested we include a mini performance from her at the events. The other talent I suggested was a very popular reality star/influencer who I had also worked with a number of times at my previous fashion company. I knew the media would be interested in talking with her and that attendees would be excited to do a meet and greet with her at the barbershop events. She was very personable and knew how to work a crowd. I also threw in that, if available, she would be relatively affordable. I watched the frowns dissipate on the clients' faces and we had a fun chat about how much they liked—dare I say loved—watching that influencer on TV.

We left with client approval for the campaign and approval to book the reality TV influencer, if she was available—and the clients really, really wanted her to be available. I texted her as soon as I got back to my desk to see if she was interested. She was but had to move some other gigs around to make it work. I got her rate for the project and, once she confirmed she was in, shared it with my team and our clients. Everyone was so happy that we sold in the idea and especially happy with me for recommending and securing the talent. I didn't know what I didn't know and had no idea that, instead of celebrating, we should have been debriefing on how to make our future pitches stronger and ensure that all members of our team could speak knowledgeably about the audiences the agency claimed to understand. But there was no debrief—no learning moments—and we just jumped straight into planning and executing: red flag #8.

For the next 12 months, I spent my time traveling across the country to client events targeting Black media and audiences, pitching campaigns to our lifestyle clients that focused on African American consumers and faking my depth of knowledge on public relations and level of experience in securing press. Over the year a few things became clear to me as I worked for this PR firm. The first was that I, along with the only other Black colleague on my team, was expected to be the expert on everything Black culture and Black media for the agency. If the client's product specifically targeted the Black community, involved a Black celebrity ambassador, or was tied to a Black-leaning cultural moment like the ESPYs or the NBA All-Star weekend, then I and/or my colleague "S" would be tapped to work on it: red flag #9. Obviously, being Black meant I had an intimate understanding of my culture, but the pressure of having to be the de facto voice for all Black people everywhere for the agency and billion-dollar brands was overwhelming at times.

But I cared very deeply about not letting brands lean into negative tropes or put out work that undermined the Black community, so I leaned into the role. I connected with every lifestyle reporter and producer at every outlet I could find that covered Black and multicultural news, entertainment, products, and culture. I learned their beats and what interested them, and I made sure they were included on all our sampling and event lists. No one had even asked if I had wanted to be *the* Black PR specialist, but I went with it because I knew that I would at least try to do right by the community.

Another thing I figured out was that I was expected to already know everything there was to know about public relations and securing media because no one there was going to teach it to me. Although everyone was nice, no one ever offered to help someone learn something new. In fact, if you mentioned you weren't familiar with something, you'd be directed to search on the internal drive for an "example of what it looks like," and no one would walk you through it or make sure you truly understood the task: red flag #10. A few weeks after I started, one of the VPs in a team meeting told me to "set up an SMT" as part of a client's new product launch. I had no idea what that acronym even meant, but after taking in the sink-or-swim vibe of the organization, I knew the right response was, "Sure."

After the meeting, I went back to my office and Googled "SMT." Once I learned it stood for "Satellite Media Tour," I researched what it was and how it worked. Turns out it is a series of scheduled interviews done in a single day from a studio or remote location with TV, radio, and digital news outlets around the country. It's a more affordable option if you want to do a ton of interviews since you don't have to fly a brand representative or ambassador around the country or book them for multiple days.

With that knowledge, I jumped on the drive to search for previous SMTs the agency had done. I found interview schedules, talking points for brand ambassadors, and invoices for the third-party SMT companies that we used. I was so clueless that I didn't even know that PR and marketing firms outsourced a lot of their work to other firms. I reached out to a few of the companies to get quotes and put together a proposal for the VP to review.

A couple of weeks later, I oversaw my first SMT. I was lucky since the brand ambassador the client selected to do the interviews was an absolute pro and had worked with the brand before. So, her on-set requests—cue cards with the messages on them in addition to printouts, a five-minute refresh break after every third interview, immediate feedback if she missed a talking point—became my template for things in the future. This process repeated itself dozens of times while I worked at the firm. They would assign me a project or task without offering any guidance or support and I would just figure it out.

I learned in those days how to listen closely. When I saw a co-worker doing something I didn't know how to do, I studied them like a scientist in a lab. No detail went unrecorded; all was saved in my notebooks for future reflection and use. Meanwhile, the community of Black reporters and journalists that I connected with were usually willing to give me real feedback on my pitches and point me to a better contact when something wasn't fit for them. This was a big deal since the press and public relations are supposed to be adversaries, as their job missions are not always aligned. Good publicists want the media to tell a good story about their clients, and good journalists want to tell the best story—and sometimes the best story isn't the most flattering for a client. But I was naïve enough to be real with them and say things like, "If this pitch is trash just let me know," and they found it endearing enough to actually want to help me. I was supposed to just be their source, but so many of them became my mentors and helped me actually become good at PR. I shouldn't have had to write my own playbook, but that's the only option on the table when one isn't shared.

Learning I needed to be my own teacher if I wanted to be successful at my job wasn't as big of an awakening for me as when I stumbled into the realization that having Black people on the team made a lot of my co-workers uncomfortable. It was comical at first. Like the time I could overhear two colleagues talking about "S" in the hallway outside my office. One of them needed to chat with her and didn't know what she looked like or where she sat. The other colleague who knew who she was attempted to describe her to him.

Co-worker 1: "She's the brunette who always smiles and has long hair. She wears dresses a lot."

Co-worker 2: "I'm not sure who that is."

Co-worker 1: "She's on the account with R. She's tall. She goes to lunch with S and J a lot."

This went on for a good two minutes when I finally called out from my office, "'S' is the other Black woman in the office." My officemate busted out laughing from behind his cubical wall. He then swung out from his chair, jumped over to me and whispered, "You can't say that": red flag #11.

"Why not? "I responded. "He was never going to find her with those vague descriptions." My officemate—let's call him Brad—just shook his head with a half-smile on his face and went back to his work. I really liked my officemate, Brad. He was a genuinely nice and level-headed person, and we liked to take walks in the morning to get bacon, egg, and cheese croissant sandwiches from the bodega on the corner. He was a kind person and clearly savvier than me since he knew how the corporate world worked. But he never told me why I couldn't say the obvious. At the time, I didn't think too much about it and just went back to whatever I was working on.

Sometimes the uncomfortableness led to new experiences, like the time one of the managing partners randomly stopped me in the hallway to congratulate me. I hadn't interacted with this agency leader before. I thanked him and added that my team had worked really hard on the client pitch, and we were really excited to win the new campaign. He smiled and said, "You've been with us for a few months now, right?" The answer was yes, but the question confused me. The amount of time he stated was so specific, and the question felt like a non sequitur—I had no idea what it had to do with the campaign pitch. And then it hit me: we were having two different conversations. An agencywide email had been sent out that morning announcing that "S" was being converted from a contractor to a full-time employee. Without thinking, I said, "Oh, I'm not 'S.' She's the other Black woman."

Embarrassment colored his face to full crimson, and he blurted out, "Sorry," turned, and abruptly walked off. As I watched him turn the corner in the office hallway, the only thought that popped into my head was, *that was odd*. I recounted the story to my officemate later that day, and I saw his eyes widen as I shared what happened. He stared at me in shock and replied, "That must have been awkward."

"Yes," I responded. "I think he felt awkward." It didn't dawn on me that I was expected to feel awkward too. It's not that I lacked empathy, but a lifetime of being placed in uncomfortable situations had left me unfazed. I just accepted it as a way of life that people might say something thoughtless to me—intentionally or not—and I would choose not to let it disrupt my inner equilibrium.

I didn't even put another thought into the exchange until a couple of days later, when I got an email from the same managing director. He had two comp tickets to the MLB World Series game for that evening but couldn't attend. He wanted to know if I wanted them. Of course I wanted them! I had only been to one baseball game in my life. It was when I was in foster care, and we sat in the nosebleed seats, and I was so small—and had such terrible vision—that I couldn't see anything that was happening on the field. I thanked him and happily accepted the tickets. I invited one of my girlfriends to come with me and snuck out of the office a little early to meet her and take the train to the Bronx. As we settled into our third-row seats of a sold-out game, she asked if the company gave out event tickets to employees often.

I told her, "Yes, but not the way I got them." I chalked it up to the partner feeling a really high level of White guilt about confusing me with "S" (red flag #12) and decided that for the evening I wouldn't dwell on it. I hadn't really had a moment to breathe since I had started working at this agency, and I wasn't about to waste this opportunity to have a night off and enjoy this once-in-a-lifetime experience with my friend. The bubbling problems would still be there tomorrow, but that night was for me. That night was about letting go, even if just for a few hours, and embracing a moment of joy without second-guessing it.

As my friend and I settled into our seats, the roar of the crowd and the bright lights of the stadium felt like a welcome escape from the stress that had been building up over the past few months. We laughed, cheered, and even indulged in overpriced hot dogs and plastic cups of wine, just like everyone else. For once, I wasn't thinking about the endless presentations, the awkward office dynamics, or the pressure to constantly prove myself. I was just living in the moment, allowing myself to enjoy something purely for the sake of it.

When the game ended—with a Yankees win—we made our way out of the stadium with the ecstatic crowd, our laughter mingling with the cheers that still echoed in the night air. The excitement around us was contagious, and I let myself be swept up in it, feeling lighter than I had in months. Sometimes, all you can do is live in the moment and move through the minefield of red flags until you figure out how to pave a new path altogether.

I didn't have all the answers, but I was beginning to understand that I didn't need to. What mattered was the decision to keep moving; to trust that with each step, I was getting closer to something better. There would still be setbacks, uncomfortable situations, and more red flags ahead, but I was learning to recognize them for what they were—and more importantly, I was learning that I didn't have to accept them as permanent parts of my journey.

CHAPTER 12
Meet Your Idols

THE LINGERING HIGH from that incredible Bronx Bomber experience turned out to be short-lived. As soon as I was back in the office, I was confronted with the reality of my situation. World Series tickets wouldn't ever be a salve for the realization that my leaders at the firm didn't actually value the work I did. All the red flags I had missed started to coalesce into a pattern of indifference that became hard to ignore. The firm just didn't seem to want to put more effort than they had to into their multicultural projects. Yes, they wanted the clients' money. And yes, they wanted the clients to believe they were experts in the multicultural space. But outside of hiring me, "S," and the sole Hispanic VP, as a firm they made no attempts to actually develop the cultural competency required to do the work really well. It was hard not to begin to take that fact personally as I was pushing myself to exhaustion, traveling across the country to execute projects with little to no support.

I worked so late in the office each evening that I had been given a key and alarm code to lock up when I left and to let myself in for early morning engagements with our campaign talent ambassadors. My holidays were spent finalizing details for brand press tours or celebrity activations. I actually spent the Fourth of July badgering a fashion house for their sketches for a custom suit we were having made as part of a red-carpet stunt for a client. We needed the suit completed right after the holiday, so I needed to get approvals in real time—which the account leads were aware of. Of course, no one responded to my emails, texts, or phone calls. When the approvals came days later, I just worked through the night for two days in a row to ensure the design was created on time. It was a one-sided relationship for sure.

Burning the candle at both ends began to take its toll on me physically and mentally. After an event I worked with one of my clients in Las Vegas, we decided to grab dinner before meeting up with some of her friends. A companion of hers met us for dinner, and while we were waiting for our food, the booming restaurant sounds grew softer and softer and then disappeared altogether.

I woke up as they were paying for the check. I didn't faint, but I had apparently laid my head down on the table in the restaurant and passed out for the duration of our meal. Luckily, my client found it amusing and kindly complimented all the work and long hours I had spent helping her execute the campaign. Part of me knew that I should feel mortified for falling asleep at a crowded restaurant while out with my client, but I was just too tired. And, when she told me to go to the hotel room and get some sleep, I'm fairly sure I smiled as I said, "Goodnight." Thankfully, my client really did value my efforts, and they never mentioned my impromptu dinner snooze to my firm. But the fact that it happened made me worried.

Another time, I heard my voice crack mid-sentence as I was on the phone, pitching a reporter to attend and cover an upcoming client event. I attempted to clear my throat and repeat what I was saying, but no sound escaped my lips. I tried again and when there was still no sound, I heard my heart racing in my ear. Terrified, I hung up on the reporter, shot them an email stating that I'd lost my voice. I sat in an airport, in a city I can't remember, and I found myself wondering if I should email the company's travel agent to book me a flight home so I could see a doctor. Worried that I would get professionally penalized if the event did not go well in my absence, I dutifully boarded the plane I was already booked on and spent the next couple of days only corresponding with my clients, reporters, talent, and bosses via email and text message. When I emailed my boss about losing my voice, I got a "that sucks" reply with a reminder to let the client know email was the best way to reach me.

A few weeks later, as I was contemplating whether this agency was the right place for me, one of my bosses walked into my office and asked me if I knew who Maya Angelou was. Did I know who she was? Did I know who *she* was? Did *I* know who *she* was? It was the craziest question I'd ever heard. It was the most ludicrous question ever posed to a Harlem native whose life was forged by trauma but found themselves still breathing on the other side. I read *I Know Why the Caged Bird Sings* in fifth grade. It wasn't assigned; I just found it in the back of our classroom and asked my teacher if I could borrow it. That autobiography was my coming-of-age solace and put into black and white what the adults around refused to tell me: that life is sometimes a long, hard journey, but you'll find yourself and reinvent yourself along the way. I re-read the book in sixth grade and again in eighth grade. Asking me if I knew who Maya Angelou was was like asking me if I knew my teeth showed when I smiled.

In the most professional tone I could muster, I responded, "Yes, I know who she is. I've read her entire series of autobiographies and have her complete collection of poetry at home." Excitedly, I threw in, "I even performed her poem, 'Phenomenal Woman,' as part of my high school public speaking class presentation."

"Great," he responded. "She's the author talent that our Chicago agency team hired to be their client's campaign ambassador for a Satellite Media Tour tomorrow. Their flights are canceled because of snow, and we want you to cover it." I'm sure my eyes widened because next, he said, "You're not going to fangirl out, are you?"

So many thoughts went through my head in an instant. The loudest was, *did you just call Maya Angelou an "author talent" like she's some sort of freelancer writer trying to catch a break?* My head was screaming, *she's not just an "author"!* She's a poet, a dancer, an actor, a singer, a civil rights activist, and a professor. She is the voice of a generation and a national treasure.

He had no idea who she was, not really, and no clue what she represented not just to Black women like me, but to the Black community and the generations of people inspired by her story.

"No, I'm not going to fangirl out," I said. I didn't have to wonder why I, a junior level employee, was being given this. "S," who was more senior than me, had been fired a few weeks before for not being a "culture fit." I knew I was the only Black person left in the office. So, I found myself standing outside the well-kept Harlem brownstone of Dr. Maya Angelou the next morning. I had gotten up extra early to stop at a bookstore on the way to her house. I had lent my aunt my copy of *I Know Why the Caged Bird Sings,* and I wanted to make sure I had one on me. I wasn't going to "fangirl out," and I wanted to make sure things went off without a hitch, but there was no way I wasn't leaving without asking one of my idols to sign a copy of one of my favorite books.

The satellite crew was already getting set up in the living room when I walked inside. I was greeted by Dr. Angelou's assistant. Dr. Angelou herself was upstairs getting ready. The crew gave me an earpiece that let me communicate remotely with the account team, who were set up in a studio in Chicago and running point. My job was to relay information from them to Dr. Angelou throughout the media tour and let her know any updates. We made really good time getting the camera, lights, and audio patched in and turning her living room into a set to conduct the interviews. We were ready to kick off the first interview and were just waiting for Dr. Angelou to come down so I could quickly review the campaign message points with her.

A few minutes later, she descended the stairs and took her spot in front of the camera. The SMT producer placed the mic on her, and I breathed a silent sigh of relief because we were going to be able to go live with the first interview on time. As a remote audio tech finished checking her sound clarity and volume, I piped in to quickly remind her of the key messages that she needed to mention during the interviews. I figured a topline highlight would be fine since we were up against time and the Chicago team had reviewed the messages with her before. I figured wrong. She let me know—in front of the client who had been sitting quietly in her living room this entire time—that she had never seen the message points before.

I was flabbergasted by this news, mainly because I'd always made sure all my talent were trained before our interviews and appearances.

I had assumed that was standard practice at our agency, but in that moment, I learned to assume nothing. I relayed this information to the Chicago team via my earpiece and—before they could make excuses or point fingers—I told them we should cancel the first interview so I could message-train her. They said, "Ok," and I proceeded to do what I believed was the fastest message training in PR history. I gave Dr. Angelou a quick background on the brand, the origins of the campaign, what we wanted consumers to do, and what we hoped they would walk away knowing. I then shared why she was the perfect person to deliver this particular message.

About 10 minutes later, we went live. The red light went on, she looked into the camera, and I held my breath, a little worried that the impromptu message training was too rushed and she wouldn't be able to remember it all. But in the end, Maya did as Maya always did from her first interview to the last. She was poetic, eloquent, and so poised: holding command of every interview, bantering with show hosts, making them laugh, recounting her work, and weaving our campaign messages in at just the right moments. I was so impressed but, more than that, mesmerized by how she could move people to lean into her every word. Even I, who was a little cynical about life and my own career in public relations, started to believe that this campaign, which I had no background on the day prior, had the potential to do real good from the inspirational way she described it.

After all the interviews were complete, we wrapped for the day. Dr. Angelou invited the client for tea in her kitchen. I waited while the satellite crew broke everything down, and when they had departed, I popped into the kitchen to say my thank-yous and goodbyes to Dr. Angelou, her assistant, and the client. While I was there, I bravely also asked her if she would sign my book.

She smiled at me and said, "Yes." She took my book in her hands and whispered to her assistant to get one of her copies. The book I had brought was a softcover version, and she said I'd probably like a hardcover signed. I wasn't sure if I had made a faux pas by buying the cheaper softcover, but I could tell she wasn't trying to make me feel bad about it. She ended up signing the hardcover she gifted me as well as the softcover, which I had her dedicate to my best friend.

Dr. Angelou gently took my hand as she handed me the signed books and whispered, "You will do well in life if you take people into your trust." I froze for a second. I'd never felt so exposed and so seen at the same time. I'd only spent a few hours in her company, but she had seen right through my nervousness, my fear, my uncertainty, my trauma, my distrust, and my hope. Her plain but piercing words felt not only like a stark contrast to the red flags and frustrations I had endured at my PR firm but also like a guide for how I needed to proceed moving forward. I didn't know what else to say, so I just thanked her for the kind advice, for the signed books and the entire day. Then I headed out to take the train to the office with her words embedded deeply in my heart.

A few months later, I found myself unceremoniously fired from the PR firm. Human Resources gave a vague explanation about me not being a "culture fit." I wasn't totally surprised since, a few weeks prior, I had provided some feedback to a press release that I knew could be taken as either constructive or uncomfortable. The press release I had been asked to review aimed at getting African Americans to enter a particular contest-like program. Since they couldn't limit the entries to just African Americans—you know, because that would be illegal—they instead opted to use language in the press release that they felt would only appeal to African American audiences. It was the most offensive piece of contemporary marketing copy that I have read in my career.

Ever the professional, I couched my feedback in sentences like, "Some people might find this offensive," and "Maybe we could explore other language," but there was no way to interpret my note as believing that press release should see the light of day. I hesitated before I hit send, but Maya's words rang in my ear. I had to take people into my trust. Either they wanted me to help them understand and grow their multicultural campaign work or they didn't. Either they wanted me to be the best at my job or they didn't. Either they trusted me to be honest with them or they didn't. The HR rep didn't provide any specific reasons or examples that led to my firing, but I'm fairly sure that email played a significant role. As he rattled off details of my imposed exit, all I heard was "you can't say that" ringing in my ear.

I'm not going to sugarcoat it: getting fired felt devasting. I would have much preferred to leave on my own terms, to say goodbye to my clients and the media contacts I made. But after the fog of professional disappointment lifted, all that was left was frustration. Frustration at the fact that I remained there after all the red flags and after it became clear that their intentions and mine didn't align. It just wasn't a place I could take people into my trust.

A few weeks later, when I started my new job—I had started applying and interviewing at other agencies soon after my awakening with Dr. Angelou—I walked into my new office wiser and with purpose. I was focused now. Focused on being in environments where I could take people into my trust or creating those environments from the ground up.

CHAPTER 13
Find Your Joy

MY FIRST JOB at 14 years old was at a summer daycare center at a church in Harlem. I liked my young charges, and my fellow teen co-workers were really nice. Our boss was another story. It didn't take us long to realize that she wasn't the biggest fan of children—or teens for that matter—and did her absolute best to avoid being near any of us at all times. While we were initially told during our pre-summer training to not be around the kids without adult supervision, by the end of the summer, parents might have been surprised to find out an actual adult even worked there.

During our time there, we handled everything from signing in the kids to devising daily activities, preparing meals, cleaning up, escorting the kids to nearby playgrounds, and ensuring the kids were ready for pickup. We essentially did everything except cut our own checks for that program. Despite our efforts, our boss perpetually wore a bad mood like a second skin. It was evident that she disliked us and her job, but we teens simply shrugged it off. Adults, we thought, were funny that way, and as long as we received our pay, we could endure her sour vibes.

Even after that first work experience it took me a considerable amount of time to realize that many people genuinely dislike their jobs. The notion of waking up early, commuting via bus, train, or car, and spending the bulk of the day in servitude to someone else makes people wish they didn't have to step one foot out of bed. They only do it because either the idea of destitution scares them or they have responsibilities they can't or are unwilling to abandon—a sobering reality of life. Most people work out of necessity, not desire. And even those who aren't weighed down by this reality and believe that people should just find a job they really love doing are confronted with another truth: Finding a job where you get to do what you love is a rarity in life for one big reason—companies are composed of people, and a lot of people suck.

I really wish my university had better prepared me for this fact. Imagine how much further along I'd be in my career if they offered a course like "Business 101: You'll Hate Your Job, but Rent Is Due," followed by "Business 201: Nepotism, Racism, and Sexism; Tips for Professionally Thriving in an Unfair Workplace" and "Business 301: Glowing Reviews but No Promotion in Sight; Knowing When It's Time to Go." Unfortunately, there was no such road map for navigating the working world and its challenges. Through trial and error, I had to painstakingly figure it out on my own. I had learned a lot about surviving within toxic companies and on unhappy teams during the early part of my corporate career, but my perspective on work underwent a significant shift during one job in particular.

After being let go from that PR firm, I did some freelance consulting for a bit before joining a new midsized agency. I had been handling a few accounts at the firm for about a year and found that my boss was pretty hands off and didn't provide a lot of direction. So, with a bit of experience under my belt, I took the initiative to create my own goals and procedures. Instead of mass-pitching client stories to every reporter under the sun, I'd call the media contacts I knew and ask them who they thought at their outlet would be most receptive to my pitch, and I'd request intros. Rather than sending large client mailers to reporters, I convinced my clients to let us send out products to a smaller group of up-and-coming digital writers and social media creators, a strategy ahead of its time in the early days of influencer marketing.

It was a challenge, but things were going well. I even secured the approval of the tiniest budget ever to promote a new independent skincare brand partnership that had been introduced in a limited number of a client's retail stores. I was the only one assigned to the project, and the client wasn't investing in any other marketing to support the skincare line. My successful efforts ended up contributing to a huge sales lift for the line. The influencer campaign was so impactful that the client rolled out the skincare line to all their stores across the country and expanded its independent brand partnership program. They also increased their budget with my agency, and my workload doubled for their account. When my boss suddenly resigned and left for another company, I was certain that I would be recognized for all my hard work with a raise or promotion. Instead, my agency did what a lot of companies do when they have hardworking talent successfully growing business: they hired a new boss to manage me.

Despite my disappointment, I wasn't bitter about being passed over. In my time at the company, I had come to recognize it as a pretty unhappy environment. Most of the employees dreaded coming every day. Senior leadership was tainted by relics from the heydays of advertising, when doing cocaine at company events was expected and sexually harassing female subordinates was actively ignored. There was an open joke that lasting there more than a few months was "a testament to your survival skills more than your work product." The place was OG toxic, but I needed to make it work. I was convinced that I already had too many job hops on my resume and that employers wouldn't take me seriously if I looked for a new job so soon after joining. And, after being fired from my first agency role for trying to do the job they hired me to do, I didn't really believe that another job would be that much better than this.

With Dr. Maya Angelou's advice imprinted in my head to "take people into your trust," I figured that having a boss who wasn't steeped in the company's noxiousness might be a good thing. I embraced her wholeheartedly, and when she invited me to lunch "to find out more about the company," I shared everything I knew—and I mean *everything*. I told her about the drugs and the rampant sexual harassment of women in the office and how HR could not be trusted. I disclosed how some of the men in the office felt comfortable touching women inappropriately and how James, who ran one of the agency's biggest accounts, was one of the biggest offenders. I shared that Sam—one of the senior leaders—seemed like a good guy and was incredibly supportive of my work on the retail account. I let her know that being scoped to billable work was of the utmost importance because everyone I knew who'd been assigned to the CEO's "non-billable" projects was fired within six months. When she asked me what my goals were, I told her, "To do good work on my accounts and get promoted." I figured that was the right answer and it was also true for me. I was honest in answering all her questions and figured I needed to try it Dr. Angelou's way. We had a great lunch and went back to the office afterwards.

Over the next few months, my high hopes were dashed. It turned out that my new boss actually had extraordinarily little marketing and advertising experience and would make the most ludicrous statements to our clients. Since she was more senior than me—reminding me often of that fact—she was expected to be at all our client meetings. Clients, however, started hinting to me that it would be ok if she didn't attend. Of course, I couldn't tell her that, since I was her subordinate and knew she wouldn't take it well. So I moved most of our client meetings to times I knew she wasn't available and would just update her after. As a result, my workload went from stressful to absolutely insane.

Instead of helping grow our current account work—as she had told me she was hired to do—she volunteered us for all the CEO's unbillable pet projects. Attending all the meetings with him solo, she would then just give me her handwritten notes with deadlines. I went from barely juggling four billable accounts with no support to having to carve out time to build out two to three new unbillable campaigns each month, in addition to my existing workload. Although my boss did all of the presenting of the campaign ideas to the CEO, she didn't put together any of the decks. I found myself working late at the office, hastily gathering insights from the internet and assembling semi-coherent strategies that never saw the light of day, all while starting to miss deadlines for my actual accounts.

More seasoned in my professionalism—and wary of being unfairly fired again—I set up a meeting with my boss to propose a solution. I pointed out that if my billable clients started to complain about missed deadlines then our department would lose its autonomy within the agency. I recommended that we bring a temp on to get some of the light daily requirements like morning media clipping off my plate so that I could ensure everything was getting out the door on time. Media clipping involved manually scanning the web, newspapers, and magazines for any new stories about our clients that we had pitched. While automated services existed, they often missed some coverage and were slow to compile reports. Our clients preferred to be updated on new coverage in the early morning, so an actual human needed to do it manually. To my surprise, my boss agreed, and two weeks later Sapphire joined our team.

Sapphire was amazing and had tons of marketing agency experience. She took tasks like sending out daily media reports to our clients off my plate and helped me stay on track with deadlines. She was a hard worker, brilliant and clearly overqualified for the small tasks she was doing. More than that, Sapphire was kind, funny, and looking for something more. We hit it off right away, and with Dr. Angelou's words still embedded in my heart, I was open with Sapphire about the company's "pain points," our boss's gaps, and my own professional desires. I took her into my trust, and it was the best professional decision I could have ever made.

With Sapphire as my co-conspirator, we were able to do even more amazing work for our client accounts. Our billable workload continued to grow as our clients became increasingly happy with our consistent successes for their businesses. At the same time, our boss leaned even more into our CEO's pet projects, enhancing her visibility within the office. She hired another temp to assist her with the work, since Sapphire and I needed to turn our attention to the growing billable account work. In another company this might have gone over better, but the pet projects continued to go nowhere, and senior leadership started to take notice of her comings and goings.

Our boss often arrived late to the office, disappeared throughout the day, and left early. A few times I watched the CEO stop by her office and open her door—without knocking—only to find it empty. The fact that he felt comfortable barging into a closed-door office of a female employee is a perfect example of the culture he fostered within the organization. Each time he did this, he'd turn to me or Sapphire and ask about her whereabouts. We'd respond, "I don't know," because she never kept us informed and we knew not to inquire. After a few months of this charade, she was unceremoniously fired. A couple of days later, one of the IT guys asked me if I wanted access to my ex-boss's email account, so we didn't miss any important client emails as they were still being notified of her departure. I told him to give Sapphire access, and she'd monitor the messages.

The very next day, Sapphire called me over to her desk to read an email she had found in our ex-boss's inbox. Evidently, our ex-boss would email herself reminders of things to do or notes that she didn't want to forget. The subject line of this particular email was "Plan of Action." The only thing I've changed in her email are the names of the co-worker and of the accounts. Everything else is printed exactly how she wrote it and read as follows:

Charell was bitter, frustrated and angry and arrogant when I came aboard; - doesn't respect anyone in the building. she said her previous boss was incompetent; she has told me she doesn't respect the CEO and that she does not want to work for James.

she has been disrespectful to me verbally, in emails and during course of business.

Sam gave her impression that she could run retail account team

I had to learn what she knew; - getting close is the best way.

fire Sapphire, hire sr account exec for 50,000 that can shadow Charell. Charell can then be fully transferred to James' team. in the interim, hire a p/t freelancer to do clip monitoring for the retail account and support for other accounts $300 week; - put that person on new account and continue to charge $60 making a bigger profit.

I'll take over the agency's biggest account and get support from the freelancer.

After finishing reading the email, I stood over Sapphire's desk and burst out laughing. My ex-boss's plan was really to learn what I did and how I did it, then take it over and transfer me to another account. Not only that, but she also wanted to fire Sapphire and hire someone cheaper to do her work. And, on top of all that, she wanted to "take over the agency's biggest account," which was run by the agency's only other female PR director, Missy, who worked in a totally separate department and had little to no interaction with my ex-boss. It's one thing to be out to get people who you think are undermining you but completely villainous to go after someone who has never even given you a side-eye. I wrote her off as a pathetic, backstabbing blunderer and went on about my day.

As the days went on, I'd catch myself thinking about that email and my ex-boss's words from time to time. At first, I'd laugh it off—after all, only a crazy person puts something like that in writing and creates a digital trail for it. But the more I thought about it, the more I realized it really bothered me, so I thought deeply about it until I figured out why. It bothered me because it was my fault she thought those things about me. When Dr. Angelou told me to take people into my trust, she never said I had to spill the tea all at once. During our first lunch, I shouldn't have been so brutally honest with my ex-boss, even though she asked. I should have been more thoughtful about what I shared and given her an opportunity to form her own opinion about the agency.

In that moment, she was a brand-new employee, probably really excited about her new role, and I basically told her she had joined a burning dumpster fire. That was thoughtless of me. Of course, she thought I was "bitter, frustrated, and arrogant." To her I probably sounded like I thought I was better and smarter than everyone at the agency. I was trying to prepare her, but she couldn't hear that because I probably made her feel like she had made a terrible career decision. In my desperation to make an ally, I forgot that how and when you say something matters just as much as what you say. I took Dr. Angelou's advice too literally and forgot that she also famously said, "People will forget what you said, people will forget what you did, but people will never forget how you made them feel."

On top of that, I had been purposefully scheduling meetings when I knew my ex-boss couldn't attend. I was doing it because I was afraid of being fired for telling her that the clients didn't want her in the meetings, but she didn't know that. And she probably figured out what I was doing and rightfully found it disrespectful. It wasn't fair of my clients to put me in that position, and I should have called them out on it and directed them to notify her or one of the senior leaders in writing that they had an issue. That would have been the more professional way to handle it. I can see how I poisoned the well with my mistakes at the start of our relationship. I own it and have learned from it. I forgive her and understand why, as a professional, she didn't want me on her team.

Now, I don't excuse her for wanting to transfer me to work under someone who I had told her actively sexually abused women on his team. Like, why not just plan to fire me? She was really going to try to put me in a situation where I could be hurt. And why fire Sapphire? She was doing really splendid work and had never done anything to offend her. And, to that point, she really wanted to steal Missy's account, who she barely knew and had never wronged her in any way, simply because she thought she could. I can see that I came at her wrong, but she clearly wasn't someone to be trusted in in any event.

Taking the time to ensure I could take people into my trust and being thoughtful about what I shared and when I shared it has been a lesson that has helped me turn some of the most trying job environments into places where I could thrive. After my ex-boss was fired, the agency re-organized our PR team of two (Sapphire and myself) under Missy. As it turns out, Missy was a genuinely kind person who had survived nearly 10 years at the agency. Once we had built a good working rapport and I knew I could trust her, I asked how she did it and she said, "I built an island."

She was exceptionally good at what she did and refused to let the corroded company culture color who she was. So, she carved out a space for herself and her team and ran it as close to an independent department as she could. Missy shielded her team members from the buffoonery, delivered high-quality work, and made herself indispensable to her clients. Most importantly, she had identified a part of her job that gave her endless satisfaction. She was a huge believer in the power of the arts, and whenever it made strategic sense she would align her clients with entertainment programs that provided resources like equipment and scholarships to up-and-coming artists and youth programs. She was under no illusions that she would make impactful change within the company, so she figured out a way to exist within it while doing good in spite of it. She turned it into a job she could love.

Watching and working under Missy changed my perception about working overall. This particular agency was pretty horrible but there was no guarantee that I would find one that was better, especially if I didn't even know which parts of what I did brought me joy. I needed to figure that out, and this dysfunctional environment was as good a place as any to do it.

So, I absorbed everything Missy told me, making mental notes of how and when to interact with senior leadership and how to communicate updates to them—often enough so they felt abreast of how business was going, but not in so much detail that they could circumvent me. Keep it professional with the men in the office who liked to overstep personal boundaries, stare dead in their eyes unamused when they made innuendos, bring a second co-worker with you into closed-door meetings, and keep conversations brief and focused on the work task at hand. Do that enough and they'll get tired of their efforts and move on to other prey, leaving you free to do your job. Build a team that you can trust, and entrust them with everything they need to get the work done well—that could be working with good people in different departments, hiring your own people, or leaning on outside vendors and freelancers who aren't ingrained in the company culture. Find the people who can help you and who you can help in return, and make them a part of your circle.

With Missy at the helm, work became actually enjoyable, and Sapphire and I were able to work on even larger accounts and projects. Things were proceeding really well until the day a co-worker from facilities popped into Missy's office and told her she needed to stop in to see the agency's lawyer, who had an office near the CEO's.

Since we had seen this happen before, we all knew that meant Missy was being fired. Missy smiled at him, told him not to take her printer because it was her personal property, and headed to the lawyer's office. When she returned, she nonchalantly told Sapphire that she had indeed been let go and then went to hunt down the facilities team who had, in fact, taken her personal printer. Once she retrieved her printer, she instructed facilities to bring a dumpster to her office. They complied and she began organizing her belongings and tossing everything that she didn't want to take with her into the dumpster. This went on for a few hours, and at the end of the day she instructed facilities not to remove the dumpster. She would be back the next day to continue her "organizing."

True to her word, she showed up late in the morning the next day and continued to sort through her files and trash anything that she didn't want to keep. She had worked for the firm for a long time and had accumulated years of files, reports, contracts, pitch decks, and client info. Though some were duplicates, many were probably the only copy in existence at the agency—but no one made a move to stop her from cleaning out her office. She took a break to take Sapphire and me out to lunch, where we enjoyed a couple of cocktails and returned much giddier than we left. Missy called it quits shortly after that and said she would return the next day to get back at it. She ended up spending five days clearing out her office files and no one made a peep about it. It was hilarious to watch senior leaders walk towards her office and hear Missy in there shuffling through file cabinets or the "bam" of a binder filled with pages hitting the side of the dumpster—and to see them turn around and walk the other way, afraid to cross in front of her threshold.

I don't remember the concocted reason they cited for letting Missy go, but the truth is no one can remain an island forever. Missy knew that and was content with simply doing as much good as she could for as long as she could and moving on when they finally realized she was never playing their game.

With Missy's departure, I was promoted and then reorg-ed under a new VP who had recently joined the agency. Smarter now, I gave the new lead space and time to absorb the agency's culture on his own, and I shared my thoughts only when he asked and when I thought he was in the right headspace to receive them. In turn he encouraged me to carve out an island—space for Sapphire and me—to continue to do excellent work. Keeping Missy's lessons top of mind, I took the time to figure out what about my job I really loved and how I could do the most good possible in the time I had. It took some soul searching and unpacking questions that I had never thought to ask myself before, like:

- *If I didn't have to work, what would I be doing?* Besides taking long weekends and drinking cocktails on a Caribbean beach,

I knew that I'd probably volunteer my time helping people in some way.

- *What bothers me most about my chosen field of PR/marketing?* It was the performative activism. Publicly, many of the brands and companies that I worked with and worked for would say they were committed to making some sort of change in the world but would do the absolute least to make it happen.
- *Is there anything likable about the company I work for?* The level of dysfunction was unbelievable but allowed me to fly under the radar and pitch ideas like my initial influencer campaign to the clients. And, although they got overshadowed, there were good people that worked there in various departments. Plus, my former boss—the one who first hired me—believed in me and created opportunities for me to show what I was capable of doing. That meant a lot to me.
- *If someone offered me a job to work somewhere else, what would they have to say to convince me to leave?* This was an easy one to answer: I wanted to be part of an incredible team that did unforgettable work.

Once I spent time with these truths, it became easier for me to see my job in a new light and take steps to make sure my work made me not only happy but also proud. I leaned into recommending campaign ideas to our client that would not only help them reach their marketing goals but also give back to the community. I tapped up-and-coming freelance writers for some of our materials, creating openings for younger professionals to get large-brand experience on their resumes. I researched and then added several small- and women-owned businesses as campaign partners, diversifying our company vendor list. As wins piled up for our clients and our budgets grew, I expanded my team, adding people filled with potential, and I gave them the cover, support, and encouragement to grow. I found out what they were passionate about and where their goals aligned with what was possible within our agency, and I plotted a plan and steered us there. Our team accomplished so many wins, executed so many unbelievable projects, and leveled up the agency in so many ways. We thrived and I loved doing my job—until the day I was let go.

Like Missy, it didn't surprise me nearly as much as it should have. After all, no one can be an island forever, and toxic jobs with toxic leaders are always going to be resistant to change. But in the time I had, I did as much good as I could, and I loved who I was while doing it. Some jobs are just trash and are designed—intentionally or not—to crush people's spirits. And changing the culture of the bad places isn't usually going to be possible. So, if you're not ready or able to leave, then you've got to be able to find joy in some portion of the work.

For me, that means taking inspiration from Missy's resilience and Dr. Angelou's wisdom and trying to do as much good as I can by creating opportunities for others wherever I can. That approach has made the work that I do easy to love and given me a professional purpose. And even when I've transitioned into new careers and roles, that purpose has remained my constant, guiding me through.

CHAPTER 14
Reinvention Is a Right

At another time in my life, getting fired—even from a very toxic job—would have made me panic. But I was further along in my career and less worried about my reputation being tarnished, since I now had multiple proof points of the amazing work I'd created and managed. I also had a decent amount of money saved up, easing the stress of finding a new role right away. But the main reason I was unbothered in the aftermath of being fired was that I had been working on building my own startup for two years and had actually gone live with the business a few months before I was let go. The day after I was sacked from my day job, I got up early and took the train to my office headquarters—a small co-working space in Tribeca—and took over answering customer calls, a task that had been handled by a freelancer since the launch day.

The business was a personal assistant agency named "PA for a Day." Essentially, it functioned as a matching service, allowing clients to connect with qualified freelancers or personal assistants (PAs) for various tasks, such as grocery shopping, furniture assembly, waiting for service people, picking up dry cleaning, or scheduling appointments. These days there are tons of options for getting help with these services, like DoorDash for groceries or TaskRabbit for furniture assembly, but when I launched it was a pretty novel concept.

Leveraging my public relations skills, I was able to drum up some rather good media coverage for the business and landed a good flow of customers from launch day. Running my own business checked all the boxes that people highlight when they talk about entrepreneurship—it was exciting, it gave me flexibility, it let me be innovative in ways that just aren't possible working for someone else, it gave me autonomy, and it was rewarding. Every news article about the company that I landed mattered because it was my company, and every client that used my services was important to me because they kept the lights on. It was special and magical and unforgettable.

But it was also incredibly hard, unbelievably stressful, and extremely expensive. And people who hype the merits of entrepreneurialism sometimes forget to mention the taxing sides of it. Succeed or fail, it's all on you. And there are way more obstacles to success than you realize when you dream of starting something new. My clients overwhelmingly loved using my services but there were still some that were difficult to please, and handling their demands consumed a significant amount of my time.

Managing cash flow, ensuring more money is coming into the business than is going out at all times, is no joke. I had to spend so much time chasing down invoice payments from my corporate clients. Often, I would have to pull money from my savings to cover the payroll when I knew the business would be in the red for the month. This, of course, caused me financial pressure since it put my ability to pay my personal expenses, like my mortgage, at risk.

As much as I liked having my own business, running it was a huge challenge and I chose to close it down after two years. Tears ran down my cheek as I sent the email to all my PAs—the freelance personal assistants who made my dream real—announcing that I was shutting down the site. There's no easy way to fail at something. All you can do is take what you learned to the next thing you do. For me, that meant being self-reflective about what I had learned about myself.

Running my own business showed me that a core value I have is to never take advantage of people. I had set a minimum payment of at least \$15/hour for my PAs because at the time that was the minimum amount considered a "livable wage." My competitors didn't pay their freelancers that amount, which is probably why their businesses lasted and mine didn't. I am just not committed to building anything deemed "successful" on the backs of struggling people.

Another thing I learned was that I loved the creative aspects of my business more than the business itself. Yes, I liked creating a solution that solved a real problem, but what I loved more was getting to tell the story and finding impactful ways to do it. I had started a company blog to share news and updates with my customers and discovered I enjoyed writing and coming up with story topics for it. I always knew I was a good writer, but it was formerly something I looked at as a task—writing letters to my mom when I was in foster care, writing press releases for my brands, writing bios for my clients. Writing the PA For A Day blog—even though it was still business related—was the first time I had just written stories. Coming up with lifestyle posts with titles like "5 Ways to Use a PA to Make Your Life Easier," "Why Asking for Help Doesn't Make You Weak," and "Best Last-Minute Gifts for Mother's Day That Your PA Can Snag Today" turned out to be fun.

As I returned to a traditional nine-to-five public relations job that paid the bills, I wanted to make sure I leveraged what I'd learned about myself, especially the creative aspect. I also rebranded my former company blog and turned it into a lifestyle blog named "Not Just a Girl in a Dress." I chose the name because of my obsession with fashion, especially dresses. On the site, I delved into topics like trending style, beauty, living, tech, and cultural news. In addition to my day job and blogging, I also started freelance writing on the same topics for well-known media publications including *MadameNoire*, *VinePair, Toms IT Pro,* and *Business News Daily*.

My foray into real journalism wasn't planned. I just happened to come across a Facebook post from an editor at *MadameNoire* looking for paid freelance writers. I figured I was a good writer and could totally write stories for a national outlet, so I sent her some samples of my work from my blog. It wasn't hubris, I just had a role model I respected that didn't believe in putting herself in a box. My aunt Merlé had worked in a bunch of different fields in her professional career—some of them were extremely cool. I knew if she could follow her passions and be successful at it, then I could too.

As I became more confident and had a substantial portfolio

of published stories under my belt, I started to pitch myself out as a "Trends & Lifestyle Expert" for TV segments. I had always had a surprisingly good eye for spotting nascent trends and liked being able to put people onto them before anyone else. I'd also always been excited by a career in television since I had worked on a TV show as an intern and seen my aunt actually co-host her own national style show. In college I had talked myself out of even exploring studying broadcast journalism because I was worried that someone might find out I was in foster care and that would derail any career I had. Going into public relations had seemed like a smarter career choice because it still allowed me to be in media and entertainment without inviting scrutiny into my past. But at this point in my life and career, I was no longer worried about being judged or looked down upon, so I wanted to see if I could land myself on television.

Using a media database that I had access to through my work in PR, I was able to easily compile the emails for the main news and lifestyle TV producers in New York City. I reached out to them to see if I could do a summer trend segment on tech or fashion. They all said, "No." Well, they didn't use that word exactly. Most didn't respond to my segment pitch email, and the ones that did replied that they'd keep my idea "in mind for the future." I knew my pitch concept was good. As a PR rep I had pitched hundreds of reporters and producers and landed countless articles and news segments for my clients. The difference now was I wasn't pitching a brand. I was pitching myself. And I was an unknown quantity as an "expert."

My aunt had long left the field of TV hosting and had landed her gig pretty unconventionally, so I didn't think she would have any advice for how I could break into the space. And I had zero TV producer connections. I figured I would need to try to network with producer contacts by joining a press association. I actually joined two and was looking online for more when I came across a Facebook post in the networking group "PR Czars." A fashion expert was looking for volunteers to model some clothes on a TV news segment she had booked. I reached out to her immediately to sign up.

The expert was a bubbly woman who had been doing fashion segments for years and was well-known in the industry. In addition to doing TV work, she worked directly as an ambassador for a couple of style brands and would act as their on-air spokesperson when they had media opportunities as well. The segment we shot was a "Spring Showers Style" theme, and a few other young ladies and I modeled trendy rainproof gear. I would hardly call myself a model—that's actually my sister's passion—but I was excited to do the segment and learn from someone who was in the field.

The expert was met at the shooting location by the news host/producer, and they talked about each look that us models wore while a camera operator captured every moment. At the end of the shoot, I quietly introduced myself to the host/producer and made small talk. She gave off a warm vibe, so I decided to shoot my shot. I told her I was a style and trends expert and wrote about everything from fashion and beauty to culture to tech. In the end, I asked if I could send her some potential segment ideas. She said she had enough style experts but would be open to some tech segment ideas. I'm fairly sure I sent her a list of pitch ideas that same evening.

Two months later I successfully organized my first TV shoot as a "Tech & Lifestyle Expert" for Fox 5, *Good Day New York*. We shot a "Summer Tech Must Haves" segment on a picturesque Manhattan rooftop. I was nervous and had to use notecards to avoid forgetting any talking points, but I secured the venue, all the awesome products from various brands' PR reps, and models to demo the products on camera while we chatted about them. I even included my sister as a model for the segment shoot because she was pursuing modeling at the time, and I thought her having a clip of herself on camera would be good for her portfolio. I made several mistakes: pulling way too many products to include in the shoot, flubbing a few lines and having to reshoot them, and not booking more time for the venue and having to quietly beg the location manager to let us finish up. But the segment looked amazing when it aired, and I relished the experience of bringing my tech trend story to life.

With that first segment as my proof point, I was able to use it to successfully pitch myself out to other networks and shows. As an official "Trends & Lifestyle Expert," I became a regular presence on local New York City shows like NBC's *New York Live* and Fox 5's *Good Day NY,* with occasional appearances on some digital shows like Marie Claire's "The Fix." The more I got to be on camera bringing my story ideas to life, the more alive I felt. Prior to each segment, I'd be worried about my lines, if tech or style products I pulled would resonate with viewers, if the host/producer joining me would like what I put together. But when that camera's red light went on everything else would fade away, leaving this natural version of me, talking about the topics I liked and savoring the moment. It was the most *real* I felt in my life when it came to work.

Except.

People get paid for "work." A dirty secret in the TV expert space is that the lifestyle, fashion, beauty, and tech "experts" or "guests" don't actually get paid by the shows for being on TV. Those women and men who you see on TV cheerfully talking about the must-have fashion or best gifts to shop this holiday season, or even being interviewed about the latest celebrity gossip or political scandals—they usually aren't paid one cent by the shows to be an on-air guest. So, all the effort that I put into organizing my segments—coming up with the themes, sourcing the shoot location, securing samples from brands, booking volunteer models, doing fittings, writing the message points and scripts, rehearsing, and taking the day off from my day job to shoot the actual segments—didn't net me any money. Plus, I would hire a freelance assistant for the shoot days to help with things like steaming clothes, shipping samples back to the brands, and capturing behind-the-scenes content to post on social and share with the brands, and I'd usually have to take an Uber to help transport all the items to the shooting location. So, each segment cost me money that I didn't make back.

Obviously, no one is going to undertake all that work without figuring out a way to make the effort worthwhile. Many on-air experts consider being on the shows a way to establish credibility and drive customers to their other business endeavors. For someone like a fashion stylist, being on TV is a terrific way to build notoriety and to land future clients. For others, the main reason to go on air is because it serves as a stepping stone to something greater.

Early into producing and doing my on-air segments, I realized that the excitement I felt when I was bringing my stories to life was unmatched. I loved being able to share the things that I cared about and do it in a way that made people happy and inspired them to try something new. I loved being on camera and, most importantly, I loved the magic of what I was able to bring to life when I was "on." I wanted to do more of it, so I looked at being an on-air expert as a pathway to becoming an on-air lifestyle correspondent, and even one day being an on-air host with my own show.

It was a big dream, but I couldn't think of a reason that I shouldn't try to make it real. I wasn't worried that there were people more experienced than me already fighting for the limited number of lifestyle TV correspondent roles available. I would just keep creating good segments, honing my skills, and trying to find the right opportunities for me. I also wasn't afraid of failing. I'd failed before and emerged stronger. If I was ever going to know if I could do this, then I needed to take the chance.

So, I kept working my day job in public relations, which increasingly felt less and less like a fit for me every day, while I kept doing my segments on the side. I wasn't ready to completely quit my day job, since I knew that more than likely any correspondent gig wouldn't be able to replace the full-time income or benefits I made there. And there were so many parts of my day job that I still loved, like building awareness for my clients and brands, but I felt creatively restricted. Where I used to love doing PR, it now felt limiting and like maybe I had outgrown the space. I knew I needed to start exploring other types of media jobs, but I wasn't sure where to start looking.

Landing a correspondent gig turned out to be just as difficult as I predicted. The roles were hard to come by and highly sought after. Whenever I'd hear about one, I'd race to send in my reel for review in hopes of scoring an audition. Most times I'd never hear back from the show, but every once in a while, I'd land an audition. I'd immerse myself in the show, its tone, its audience, the type of stories that they covered, and the style of the current hosts and correspondents. During auditions, I'd try to keep the energy high and try to keep the tenor of the show in mind as I read lines from the teleprompter. The auditions always seemed to go well but they never seemed to lead to a callback.

The few times I was able to secure feedback on my audition, the responses revolved around my appearance, with comments like "you don't have the look for TV" or on my lack of notoriety and social media followers.

It's hard not to feel frustrated when you're being vulnerable, putting yourself out there, and not getting anywhere. But I tried to stay positive, looking at each audition as a learning experience and an opportunity to get better where I could. And honestly, with each audition I went on, I did get a little better; my teleprompter reading became smoother, and I was able to add emotional intonation to match the words flowing on the screen. Ad-libbing became more natural, allowing me to maintain the flow of segments when the teleprompter stalled or the next story wasn't loaded correctly. So I decided to focus on what I could control. I couldn't change "my look," and quite frankly, I didn't want to. It took a long time for me to like the person I am, and I was happy with me. But I could try to improve my "notoriety" and social media numbers. So, I started creating more content and posted more consistently with the hope of increasing my follower count.

I also knew that being the best and being known for being the best are two different things. If I wanted people to think of me as an on-camera storyteller, then I had to get them talking about me in that way. Drawing from my experience in public relations representing brands, I knew the best way to get people talking was to already be part of the conversation. So, I hired my own publicist to help generate some publicity around me and the work I did. My publicist, Kayla Rose—such an awesome name—was just starting out her PR business and looking to show the world what she could do. She was young, creative, kind, and driven; she reminded me of myself when I embarked on my career, and I figured I could share what I knew about securing media coverage with her, giving us an edge.

As it turns out, she didn't need very much from me in terms of guidance. Pretty early on she worked her magic to get me on the invite lists for a number of New York Fashion Week shows and red-carpet events and landed me interviews on a bunch of podcasts and in smaller media outlets. As time went on, she was able to get me quoted in larger digital and national publications, and I was all too happy to share my thoughts on the latest fashion trends or dispense career advice. When I needed to go dark because I was working on a big campaign or traveling for events for my day job, she used the time to plot out the next wave of pitches or to help to land me trend segments for when I returned. Entrusting my personal brand and dreams to a relative stranger should have been terrifying, but any and all worries about someone else not caring about my goals as much as I did were laid to rest by the efficiency I gained from having Kayla's help. There is so much truth to the adage that you can go further and faster together than you can go alone.

With the increase in media coverage that Kayla was able to secure, I stopped receiving feedback about my "look" and even heard less hemming and hawing about my social media numbers, which had grown (albeit not drastically). And the more I moved forward with my TV journey, I realized that being in front of the camera was just one of the ways I could tell great stories. Up until then I had been struggling to reconcile my career in public relations with my work in TV—until I finally admitted that they didn't align.

Accepting this realization and figuring out what to do about it were two different issues. In the years that I had been learning everything I could about TV hosting, producing, and visual storytelling, I had moved from one PR role to another, never quite finding the right fit because no matter how I contorted myself to get the work done, I simply didn't fit. I struggled with this reality for a while and finally started to look for roles outside of public relations but still in the world of media and advertising. Perhaps, I reasoned, there was a way to bridge the gap between my side hustle and my day-to-day work. I had no idea what that new role looked like, but I cast a wide net. In addition to applying to various roles online, I also reached out to my old bosses and friends in the industry to let them know I was looking for a new opportunity outside of PR. My best jobs had always come through contacts and referrals anyway, so seeking help with my search made sense.

As it turned out, a friend and former colleague I had managed reached out to tell me about an opportunity at the ad firm she was with. She was working at one of the top 10 advertising agencies in the country in a department that focused on building awareness for their clients through innovative content and storytelling. They were specifically on the hunt for a director with experience in the production and video media space, covering broadcast TV, streaming, and social platforms. This role was for a brand I had worked for in the past, and some of my old client contacts were still with the company so I would have relationships already in place. The role sounded ideal, and I jived with the team when I went in for my interviews.

A few weeks later, I found myself fully immersed in a role that seemed tailor-made for my passions and expertise. The role took me across the country, overseeing the orchestration of commercial shoots, TV and film integrations, and live events that artistically brought my ideas to life. Collaborating closely with audio partners, I also delved into the realm of sponsored podcasts.

My journey had come full circle. The role felt like a natural extension of myself, allowing me to indulge in the art of storytelling that had always resonated with me and leverage the different media segments I'd now spent time in. I found my stride: balancing my hard-won on-camera charisma with my advertising acumen. This alignment was considered particularly useful for my clients and agency. My ability to discern and capitalize on emerging trends, combined with my presence on local and national television shows, was an asset in the world of advertising. Finally, I fit in.

Having someone with positive media buzz and "notoriety" associated with their brand was appreciated by my clients and agency. They would send notes of congratulations whenever they happened to catch one of my segments on TV. Their support made it clear that this uncharted career journey that I was on didn't have to be traveled in secret. It was also clear that I was now a rarity in the industry. Looking ahead, I didn't know if this path would lead to me developing and hosting my own shows, but I was excited to keep blazing my own trail and evolving in a career that made me smile.

CHAPTER 15
The Protagonist Is You

When I was really young, there was only one career I dreamed of having: to be a singer like Janet Jackson. Unfortunately, my dream was dashed by two sad realities: one, that there could only ever be one Janet. The woman is a legend. And two, that I can't carry a tune to save my life. As I got older and accepted that being a popstar princess wasn't in my future, I started to align myself to more tangible career goals. What I wanted to be continued to evolve with each year—a music producer, a TV host, a publicist—but my plan for getting there never wavered. I was so motivated by the steps of going to a good high school, then a good college, then getting a great job, and having an awesome place to live that I never even considered what the other elements of my adult life could look like. I was focused on moving forward and leaving the memory of my time in foster care behind me.

So, I didn't put too much stock into a random moment when an attendee at a work training I had given asked me if she could have my number to give it to her son, who was about my age. She was an elementary teacher and seemed nice—and swore her son was a nice guy—so I said, "Sure," gave her my number, and didn't think any more about it. I'd dated a few guys in college and early on in my career, but I never really clicked with anyone. Having a boyfriend and then a husband and family seemed like something I should want, but it really wasn't something I spent a lot of time thinking about. Leaning into work was my priority—the easy place to focus—because I felt my career trajectory was something I could choose.

Her son called me a few days later and we ended up going out. True to her word, he was really nice, funny, and cute, and we shared an appreciation for the TV show *Family Guy*. We dated for a couple of weeks when he surprised me with a T-shirt he had come across featuring one of the show's characters. I said, "Thank you," but the gift triggered me in a way that I couldn't put into words at the time. He had given it to me to be nice, but my mind couldn't shake the idea that he was really just giving me something so I'd owe him something in return. The idea that he might be trying to manipulate me with kindness to get something from me was too much for me to emotionally process.

We went on a couple more dates, but I couldn't shake that anxious feeling about him and decided to simply stop returning his calls. After his third attempt at reaching me, he left me a heartfelt voicemail saying that he felt like I was ghosting him—I was—and he wasn't going to call again. I felt awful. I didn't mean to hurt him, but I couldn't figure out why being with him suddenly made me feel so uneasy.

Instead of calling him back and talking it through, I called my BFF and shared my self-created crisis with her. After listening to me recount the details, she paused and asked me in a calm tone, "So… *why* are you ignoring him?"

Believing she just wasn't getting it, I replied, "I don't know. Maybe my family just screwed me up."

She paused again and then, without taking a breath, said, "You know you can't blame your family for every issue in your life. You're not a kid anymore. Maybe you should see a therapist." If anyone else had said that to me, I would have brushed them off, but I trusted no one in the world like I trusted my best friend. And hearing her tell me that I needed to take responsibility for my choices and for my life hit me like an express train. All I could respond with was, "You're right."

Keeping myself busy with work and my career goals had allowed me to ignore the anxieties and unhealed wounds that I had buried deep. It wasn't until my BFF called me out for pushing a kind person out of my life that I paused to admit that the trauma from my childhood was still a part of me. In that moment, I committed myself to taking responsibility for the decisions I made and doing my best to understand why I was making them. If something triggered me, I started being honest about feeling anxious and telling people the truth about how I felt, even if it made them uncomfortable.

This made for some awkward encounters over the years, like one time when I was at a friend's game night and one of her guests' mean-spirited outbursts at losing a card game made me uncomfortable. Instead of sitting in my discomfort, I said directly to the guest, "You're making this unfun for me so I'm going to go play one of the other games." Everyone at the table went silent as I got up to join another table of guests playing a different game, but I felt good about deciding not to let myself remain in a situation that would ruin my evening.

Over the years, I've gotten even more comfortable in owning my choices and can proudly say that I never shamefully ghosted a guy again. Anytime I felt really uneasy in a relationship, I would have a conversation with the person about why and try to be thoughtful in my words as I explained that I didn't want to continue dating. Being honest with the things that didn't sit well with me helped me be more honest with myself about the things I really needed in a relationship. The clearer I became in knowing what I needed from someone else, the clearer I became in seeing what I needed from myself. If I were going to truly take responsibility for myself and understand my triggers and wounds better, then I needed to talk with someone about it. I took my BFF's advice and sought out a therapist.

I wish I could say that finding a therapist that I felt comfortable with was easy, but it was actually an annoying multi-year process. When I first started my search, my work insurance didn't cover therapy at all. Then when I got a new job—and better insurance—it only covered a limited number of sessions with therapists I didn't feel could relate to my background or experiences. Finally, after a lot of internet research, I found a practice that seemed like it was geared to people, like me, who survived tumultuous childhoods and worked in taxing environments. Of course, they didn't accept my insurance, so I had to pay out of pocket for my sessions. I reasoned my mental wellness was a bigger priority than my hair appointments, so I was willing to invest in it as such.

For months, I met with my therapist in person weekly as I recounted stories from my work and personal relationships that I felt were worth talking through. On some occasions, my therapist would give me advice or an exercise to navigate how I could make peace or move on from the situation, but most times she would say something along the lines of "that sounds like a good way to think about that." I usually left feeling glad to have talked with someone neutral about my challenges, but it was never the fully cathartic feeling that you hear people mention when they are speaking about therapy. About a year into our weekly visits, my therapist opened with a different question than her regular, "Tell me about your week." Instead, she opened with, "We've been meeting for a while, and it seems like you have everything together and have a good outlook on life. So, tell me why you're *really* here." Before I could respond, she continued, "You've shared a lot of personal history with me, but I think there are things you want to share but haven't."

If I hadn't spent the year with her and getting a feel for the type of person she was, I might have deflected her question or said there was nothing else I wanted to talk about. But I had spent the last 12 months watching her take notes during key parts of the stories I shared, pausing me to ask questions and circling back each week to follow up on if I had tried the advice or exercises she had shared, or if my feelings on the situations had changed. I knew she was taking the time to get to know me and was certain she was waiting for a time when she thought I felt safe enough to go deeper. The time she invested let me know I could trust her, and when she asked the hard question, the stories that I never wanted to breathe life into tumbled out of me.

I told her about my childhood in foster care and living with family members. But really told her about it this time. The beatings that happened when I was *bad* and the ones that happened when I knew I hadn't been "bad" at all. How I would shrink into myself to try to stay off the radar and avoid getting hit. I told her about the "good son" of one of my foster parents who would wait until everyone was asleep to sexually abuse me at night. I told her I felt shame for letting it happen and small because I knew I wouldn't be believed. As the tears streamed down my face, I poured out my resentment over the things that people who were supposed to protect me saw happen but actively ignored. I told her about how I knew I was made to feel like nothing more than a paycheck and a burden and how angry I was at my family, at the system, at the world for making me carry all this weight. And finally, I admitted how guilty I felt for having survived. I told the unedited story of my early life for the first time in all its painful detail, unafraid.

She listened and leaned in, handing me tissues from a box often, and then finally handing me the entire box. And, when I was done with my rambling of revelations, she said, "You were a child; none of that was your fault." It's not something I hadn't told myself a thousand times, but it landed different coming from someone I trusted who held space for all of me. As she and I continued to talk, my tears stopped flowing, my breathing became easy, and for the first time I listened as someone told my story back to me. "*You get to be angry about what you went through. You didn't deserve any of that; you deserved better. And you have to celebrate yourself, really celebrate yourself, for all you achieved in spite of all the pain. You have to say the words, 'I'm proud of myself.'*" She asked me if I believed that. I said I did because I really did feel proud of myself. And then she told me to say the words. "I'm proud of myself," I said softly, and then I said it again, louder this time: "I'm proud of myself."

Thus began my focused work of unpacking the stories that were weighing me down on my journey of becoming the person I wanted to be. The moments that I needed to wade through so I could better understand not just what my triggers were but why they existed. The other stories may have been easier to relive, but these were the memories that I needed to set free.

The more I sat with the moments, the more I replayed them, the less they actually brought me pain. The more I thought about them, the more I admired myself for coming out the other side. I deserved better as a child, and I'm proud of myself for recognizing that now and for building a life for myself that is rooted in unshakable self-love. The self-work is not over—healing takes time—but I no longer have stories I'm afraid to tell. And, when I think about the stories I want to leave behind, the one thing more than anything I want people to know about me is: *she survived the worst but was brave enough to still respond to the world with kindness.*

PART III
Thriving, Living & Loving

CHAPTER 16
Repay In-Kind

PEOPLE WHO SAY "money doesn't buy happiness" clearly have never had to choose between buying a pushcart hotdog for lunch or a subway pass so you don't have to walk four miles to get home at night. Trust me, my stomach and feet would have been much happier if I could have eaten and then also taken the train. Money, or lack of it, has played a hand in much of my life. What I would have given to be able to go to the Land of Make Believe amusement park with the rest of my elementary class or do more than browse at the Scholastic book fairs. Belittling the importance of money in our lives is honestly pretty disrespectful. Not just because it trivializes people who weren't lucky enough to have been born with it, but also because it undervalues all the important things that money provides access to, like opportunities, choice, safety, and yes, happiness. Money has the power to transform lives.

It changed mine.

It's crazy when I think back on it, but the factor that decided whether I went to college wasn't my grades, which were good, or my extracurricular activities, which were many, or my ability to write a compelling essay—I don't remember what I wrote but I'm sure it was decent. No, the determining factor on whether I went to college was $50 for an application fee that I did not have. I made it to my senior year of high school with excellent grades, accolades for my tennis achievements, double the yearly volunteer hours required by my school, and I still fell short. Even though I had spent every free moment each semester either babysitting for my teachers' young kids, working in the on-campus convenience store, or managing the computer lab to pay for all the things my scholarship didn't cover, I didn't have enough money remaining to pay the $50 for my college application fees by the due date.

I knew I couldn't ask for the money from my family and wasn't sure what to do. So, I went to talk to my college counselor, Sue Iverson, about it. Embarrassed, I started to bring up how much I was short, hoping there was a grant of some sort that I could apply for, when she cut me off. She told me she'd already paid the fees when she submitted my applications, and I could pay her back whenever I could. I never could. And she never mentioned the topic again. Without those fifty dollars I wouldn't have graduated high school, since getting accepted to college was a requirement to graduate from my boarding school. I wouldn't have gone to Boston University, made the friends I made, and learned life could be fun. I wouldn't have studied abroad in London and experienced the magic of Paris. I wouldn't have had the space I needed to gain perspective to see the generational curses that I needed to break and the baggage that wasn't mine to carry. Fifty dollars from Sue Iverson changed my life. Fifty dollars—and a kindhearted person—opened the door and made it possible for me to walk through.

That wasn't the only time when cold hard cash made it possible to accelerate my life. Growing up in foster care and run-down apartments made me dream big of owning my own home someday: a place in the city, my city, where I felt safe, that I could decorate however I wanted, and that no one could take from me. After I graduated college, I started researching the cost of condos and houses in NYC and put together my plan to one day own one. In addition to my day job, I worked after hours as a beverage sampling consultant, AKA a "shot girl" for different liquor companies in the city. I'd hand out free samples or shots of liquor to patrons at clubs, restaurants, and liquor stores at night and on weekends. I'd made between $20 to $30 an hour doing this, and that was the money I squirreled away into my future home fund. I snuck out early from every single one of my day job's evening happy hours, but I managed to save around $30,000 doing my part-time gigs over a few years, which was more money than I had ever had.

In the course of my research, I also stumbled across a city-sponsored housing grant program that gave $20,000 down payment grants to first-time home buyers in New York City. The only catches were that you had to sign up for a series of in-person financial literacy classes, you had to buy a home in a "revitalizing area of the city," and you had to be able to put down at least 20% of the home cost—inclusive of the grant—at the time of purchase. It took me a year of nonstop calling to secure a spot in the financial literary class, but at the end of the three-night course, I walked away with a very unofficial-seeming, clip art-looking certificate that guaranteed me $20K towards my closing costs.

The grant certificate was good for two years, and I figured it would take me that long to find a decent and affordable place in the city. I got pre-approved at a bank for a mortgage, secured a real estate agent, and started my search. Each week the agent would send me a list of places, and I'd meet her to visit them on the weekend. We started our search in Harlem because that's the part of the city I grew up in and I always felt comfortable there. Quickly it became clear that "revitalized" Harlem was beyond my budget. I was pre-approved for around $500,000 but I knew I would struggle to pay a monthly mortgage that high, so I really wanted to find a place for between $250,000 and $300,000. Nothing my agent could find in Harlem was less than $450,000, and they were even smaller than the apartments that I grew up in. So we expanded our search to Queens, which is the borough I was living in at the time.

I started sending my agent places I found on online listings that I wanted to see because she didn't know the Queens area as well as Manhattan. Queens is more than four times larger than the island of Manhattan and much of it isn't served by the subway. I really needed to find a place close to public transportation so I could get to work easily every day. We went to see a ton of places and all of them were awful. One place was so disgusting that I refused to even cross the threshold into the roach carcass-filled living room. Early in our Queens search I had seen a cute place advertised that looked like a scam. The image of the space was too bright, looked too clean and too spacious. I was sure it was a bait-and-switch. As the prospects of available properties dried up and as we started to close in on the end of my first year of my two-year grant window, I sent her the listing and she set up a tour.

I hopped off the 7 train and walked the two blocks to where the apartment was located, fully expecting to see a run-down building in complete distress. Instead, I was greeted by a newly constructed condo building that was warm and inviting. We entered the building and rode the large elevator to the third floor and walked into the available apartment. To the left was the small but well-appointed kitchen, inclusive of a stainless-steel fridge, microwave, dishwasher, and stove. I'd never lived in a home with a dishwasher and wasn't expecting it to be in any home that I could afford. The kitchen had a marble island countertop that opened onto the nicely sized, well-lit living room. Off the living room was a glass door that opened to a private balcony that was large enough to fit a bistro table and some chairs. Flanking the living room on opposite walls were the doors to the two bedrooms. The larger of the two rooms was big enough for a queen bed with plenty of floor space left over, and it had a good-sized closet by New York standards. The second bedroom was smaller but could still fit a queen bed, and it had two decently sized closets. The bathroom was big with all-marble tile and a large tub. I thought the sink was too big for the space and the light fixture above the mirror was a brassy nightmare, but those were my only complaints so far. The building also had a laundry room, gym, and garage. It was as near perfect as could be, so I told my agent to make an offer before we left the tour. It was soundly rejected.

The building owner wanted to get at least the full listing price of $290,900 for the condo and it was the last one for sale in the building. I knew I could afford the monthly payments, but that sale price would push the required down payment to around $60,000, and I only had $50,000 between my savings and the city grant. I was short $10,000, and not having enough money when you need it feels the same as having no money. I resigned myself to the fact that I was going to lose out on the perfect place and called my best friend, Schnell, to lament and distract myself from my grief. I dished about the perfectly pretty condo that I couldn't afford, and she asked me how much I was short.

I huffed out, "Ten thousand dollars," and she said nonchalantly, "I can loan that to you. Just pay me back."

I'd met Schnell on my first day of college. She was a sophomore and lived directly across the hall. Full of southern charm and a thousand-watt smile, a warm energy just seemed to surround her. I don't remember if she introduced herself to me or if I said hi first, but I do remember that not long after meeting her I walked into her room and hopped on her bed to chat her up. Part of the reason I remember that is because at least once a year she brings up that one time I sat on her clean sheets with my dirty outside clothes on. We've been sisters since that moment, and to this day, I do not allow outside clothes on the bed.

Schnell's upbringing was different from mine in many ways, yet there were enough similarities that we've always understood each other. Her dreams of building her own version of adulthood were as big as mine and she worked even harder than I had to make them a reality.

That's why I knew she was sincere in her offer to loan me the money I needed for the down payment. She had purchased her own place, a cute townhouse in Georgia, about a year earlier after working and saving for years. I was proud of her and always excited to hear her decorating updates. I knew she wanted the same thing for me. So I didn't hesitate to accept her kindness, and two weeks later, my offer on the condo was accepted. The first thing I did when I moved into my place—after buying a new bathroom light fixture—was place an ad for a roommate to lower my personal monthly costs. It took a little over a year, but having a roommate made it possible for me to pay Schnell back faster than I expected.

At 26, my condo wasn't the first place that I lived in as an adult, but it was the first place that felt like mine. Every wall I painted, every picture I hung on the walls, and every piece of furniture I lugged from Ikea and painstakingly put together myself was the actualization of a promise I made to myself a long time ago. Schnell gave that to me—well, she and her $10,000 did—and I am forever grateful to her for providing me with the opportunity to obtain what I wanted most in life: a home. It's her gift and Sue's that I keep top of mind now that I'm in a place in my life where I have the resources to enable opportunities for others. I can't always help monetarily—I'm far from rich—but when I can, I do, because I know that people can't walk through doors that aren't open.

Money isn't trivial. Not having access to it can hold people back, delay promise, and hinder aspiration. People who are lucky enough to never have to worry about affording their happiness should remember that. And those unlucky enough to know the uncomfortable hardship that is financial insecurity should never feel ashamed of having to prioritize immediate needs over future dreams. But never let a temporary monetary reality stop you from planning to take your next step forward if and when a door is opened for you. And, if you find yourself in a position where you have the ability to open a door for others, pay it forward.

CHAPTER 17
Do It Afraid

Nearly everything everyone has told me about overcoming my fears is wrong.

"Never show your fear; just try it, and you won't be afraid; they're more scared of you than you are of them." That's not quite right.

In my experience, what people often misunderstand about fear is that it's not a quirk to be ignored or stamped out. And if you're going to address it, you need to respect it.

Fear most certainly doesn't manifest from nothing. A lot of fear stems from trauma, shame, disappointment, or the anticipation of it. You can't simply pretend it doesn't exist. It takes root from life experiences—sometimes ones we can't even remember. Fear has a purpose. It exists to keep us safe, to prevent us from engaging in activities that may cause harm. Fear is sometimes comforting. It's easy to understand because it's honest. And we listen to it because it's one of the most helpful expressions of what we feel.

I was terrified of dogs most of my life. Big dogs. Little dogs. Friendly dogs who just wanted to be petted. All of them caused a shockwave through my spine: a heart-on-fire, verge-of-tears type of fear. It was never a mystery to me where the terror began. In one of the foster homes I lived in as a little girl, my foster parents used to threaten to let their dog bite me. They would yank me out into the yard, press my body up to the fence where their big German shepherd was kept, and hold my face against the links while the dog barked and growled. I'd cry and scream, but they'd just laugh and tell me they were going to let him bite me if I was bad. I carried that fear—that trauma—with me for most of my life. I'd tense up whenever a dog was near me and go out of my way to avoid them. I'd cross the street to stay out of the path of a leashed one and would change course altogether if I spotted a canine without a leash.

As I got older, my anxiety grew. It wasn't only because of my fear of dogs but also because of my fear of having to explain to dog-loving friends and co-workers that I didn't want their pet anywhere near me. Apparently, people take that personally, and I do get it. For a lot of people dogs aren't just pets; they're companions and even an extension of family, so not wanting to be near someone's dog can easily be misread as not wanting to be near them. To be honest, as much as I feared dogs, I could never actually bring myself to hate them. One time, I saw an evening news report about a house full of neglected and abused dogs that were rescued, and I remember feeling so bad for them and thinking only the worst type of person could do that. I wish I could say that by then I'd already come to terms with my fear, but it wasn't until years later that I was able to unpack my trauma.

The moment that brought me face-to-face with my fear and helped me start to move forward is a funny one. After covering style and tech trends on local news shows for a couple of years, my publicist, Kayla, called me to tell me she had gotten me something big. It was a national booking on the Harry Connick Jr. talk show, which was a huge opportunity. I had never been on a national show as a lifestyle expert before, so I was excited about this. It was exactly what I needed to move to the next level in the industry.

One of the biggest quirks about being a "lifestyle expert" is that, usually, to land a permanent recurring correspondent gig with a national TV show, you must already be making regular appearances on national shows so that you can demonstrate your expertise and ability to build a following. So, to be on a national show, you already have to have been on a national show. A total catch-22. What really happens, then? People in the industry get around this by knowing the right people and having the right connections. I didn't have either, so this opportunity was too big to pass up.

There was a challenge, however. The fashion segment was for Halloween. Not a problem—I love everything about Halloween: the parties, the costumes, the ability to be someone else for a while—maybe even the person you've always wanted to be or admire the hell out of. But this was a "best costumes for your pet" segment, and the "pet" part was the issue. I'd have to be on set with dogs and actually engage with them. Somehow, in the entire time of working with my publicist I had managed to never mention that I was terrified of dogs. It hadn't been something I thought to share but, in hindsight, it was something that I should have brought up. Yeah, you know, the four-legged creatures that bark? They petrify me to the point of tears. It's probably better if we avoid segments that include them. I just never considered that this situation would ever come up, so here I was.

I was faced with an impossible choice: pass on the segment and risk *never* landing a national segment opportunity again, or do the segment and possibly be so paralyzed with fear of being bitten that I bomb and never get invited to another show. I was afraid of doing it and afraid of not doing it. After agonizing for a few hours, I finally landed on a question that helped me decide what to do: are you more afraid of trying and failing than of never knowing if you could do it at all? Could I respect my fear—honor it, even—while still making space for something else?

After taking a deep breath, I decided to take the opportunity in front of me. The truth was that my options would always be limited if I didn't expand to national shows, and this was the only national opportunity that I had. The prospect of missing out on a potentially career-altering opportunity outweighed the fear that threatened to hold me back. All I could do after saying yes was hope that if I failed—and embarrassed myself on national TV—I'd fail forward.

There was about a week between me confirming my appearance and the show taping, and I spent it with my stomach in my throat. I was worried I'd freeze up on set or wouldn't be able to remember my lines or would start crying if a dog ran up to me. As bad as the week leading up to the show was, the morning of the taping was even more stressful. The show hadn't sent me the script until the night before, so I was pretty rusty with the lines. I had always written my own scripts for my segments, so I didn't even realize I'd need to memorize theirs until it landed in my inbox. The producer did a run-through with me without any of the dogs on set, but I was so nervous trying to recite the script from memory, I couldn't pronounce the various breeds of dogs correctly. I could see the producer becoming frustrated as the rehearsal went on. It's hard to say "shih tzu" when you've got a crippling fear of one jumping in your lap and the added pressure of knowing this is a make-or-break moment in your life.

After the morning rehearsal, the producer walked me to the green rooms where the various dogs and their owners were waiting for the show to start. I didn't want the producer to know I was afraid of the dogs, so I stepped into each green room—there were about six in all—and said hello to the owners while keeping one eye on the potential terrors in the room. Luckily, the dogs were all well-trained, and none of them came near me or barely glanced my way.

Once the producer brought me back to my dressing room, I ran my lines over and over until it was time to do the actual taping. About an hour later, the producer came to walk me to the stage. As we moved through the hallway, I closed my eyes and took a deep breath, let it out, and smiled. I was still terrified, but at least I could still move my feet forward. On set, they sat me down next to the show host, Harry Connick Jr., who graciously introduced himself and welcomed me to the stage. The red light went on, and he opened the segment and introduced me to the audience, and I didn't completely blow it.

I want to be clear: this isn't a clean narrative of facing your fears to master them. I didn't that day. I rushed some of my lines, looked down at my cue cards way too often, and slightly died a little inside each time my voice cracked as I was speaking. But I made it through. I did feel my face get hot when the first costumed dog hit the makeshift runway—which was a good distance from where Harry and I were seated—but still, I managed to highlight the key facts about each of the costumes the parade of dogs modeled. Before I knew it, we were closing out the segment. The red light flicked off and three of the longest minutes of my life were over. I thanked Harry and was guided off set by the producer. He told me I did a good job, and although I didn't believe him, I thanked him.

While we were waiting for the elevator to take me to the lobby so I could depart the studio, one of the dogs from the segment was brought out by his owner. I don't remember the breed, but he was the largest dog that modeled in the segment. I stared down at the dog, and, turning his head, he stared back up at me. In that moment, I did something I never thought I'd do.

I kneeled next to the dog and began to pet him. He was fluffy and breathing calmly and didn't flinch at all while my shaky hand brushed his fur. It was the first time I'd ever actually pet a dog. The producer asked if I wanted a picture, so I handed him my phone. He snapped a few pics before the elevator door opened. When it did, I popped up and said goodbye to the producer, the dog owner, and even the dog. I didn't master my fear that day, but I didn't have to. I just needed to open up to other feelings, too.

A few months later, I came across a casting call for a national hosting opportunity for a new streaming network: AKC TV, or as it is better known, American Kennel Club TV. I reached out to the job poster and sent over a copy of my Halloween Costumes for Pets segment, and they brought me in for an audition. I wasn't certain if they had dogs on set as part of the audition but figured if I could fight my fear once, I could do it again. Still, I was super relieved when I arrived on set and there wasn't a fluffy four-legged being in sight. The audition went as close to perfect as an audition could go—I flawlessly read the teleprompter script, got my "guest" to laugh during the mock live interview, and stayed cool and collected on camera as the tech failed during the mock video interview. In the end, they hired someone who had more on-camera experience and was already hosting a show for another network. But they liked me so much they offered me a recurring correspondent gig with them. I was all too happy to accept.

In my years working for the network, I slowly started to move through my fear of dogs. I never let on that I was terrified—that seemed like a surefire way to get fired. But with each shoot, I got more and more comfortable working with dogs, and my fear faded more and more. In two years, I went from never having petted a dog to rolling on the floor with them and having a good time. Life is funny this way. I'm not totally cured of my fear of dogs. When a stranger's dog comes bolting towards me in a park or on the street, my heart still skips a beat. But the fear isn't debilitating anymore. I just take a breath and keep on moving, and sometimes I even give them a soft pat on the head for good measure.

Being an official correspondent opened other doors for me too. I was able to expand into other paid opportunities such as hosting events, moderating panels, keynote speaking, and brand sponsored social media posts. This financial boost allowed me to cover not only Kayla's monthly retainer from my TV-related activities but also essential expenses like updating my hosting TV reel and establishing a website showcasing a portfolio of my best work.

If I've learned anything from my journey with dogs, it's this: you don't have to overcome your fears, and you don't have to deny them. They're part of you. But if fear is keeping you from doing what you want in life, then just do it afraid. The fear is a part of you, sure. But you might find out—as I did—that it's not the only part.

CHAPTER 18
Show Up Whole

EARLY IN MY career, one of my bosses would tell all of us wide-eyed, impressionable, entry-level employees that we needed to "check our baggage at the door." He went on to elaborate that being able to separate your personal problems from your work life was the hallmark of a truly successful professional. I believed him. As a vice president at the company, he made a lot of money, and all the clients and senior staff seemed to respect him. He also had a lovely home—I never saw it, but he spoke proudly of it—and a wife and kids that he'd mention from time to time. He had the life that I aspired to have, so I took his unsolicited advice seriously.

It would take me years to figure out that his advice—his approach to being successful—was limiting. It wasn't necessarily wrong; it had worked for him, after all. But it wasn't whole. If all I wanted in life was to grow in my career just so I could make the most money, then hiding away a part of myself so that I could be viewed as the consummate professional made sense. I tried to build my career that way for a while. But the more I advanced, the less satisfied I felt about the person I was pretending to be. So much effort was being invested in actively hiding the "problem" parts of me—my time in foster care, my unconventional family, my trauma, my triggers, my mental health needs—that I was suffocating the person I had the potential to be.

I wish I could say that I had an epiphany and came to the realization on my own that my attempt at chasing someone else's version of success was actually holding me back, but I didn't. Instead, that personal awareness was awakened by a mundane occurrence that forced me to admit that I couldn't afford to hide who I really was.

One morning while perusing the news, I came across an article that completely shook me. New York City was considering cutting the budget of a nonprofit that provided free advocates to kids in foster care, and the organization was trying to get the administration to reconsider.

If it had been any other group in peril, I might have just skimmed the story and moved on to the next article. But it wasn't. It was kids in foster care that they were seriously considering depriving: kids who were ripped from their families, from their homes, from their communities and their friends. Kids who had their belongings tossed in trash bags and were bounced from foster home to foster home. It was kids who'd already lost everything important to them in life, and now grown adults were callously considering cutting them off from advocates who were volunteering to help them. It was kids who were struggling to hold onto hope and were wondering if quitting life would be easier. It was kids who were like me, living the life I'd lived.

With my face wet with tears, I fired off an impassioned impromptu letter to the editor of the news outlet thanking them for writing this story and asking them to try to keep the pressure on the administration, so they didn't cut the budget for the nonprofit. Next, I shot over my first email ever to the Mayor's office and told them how important it was to not cut resources to vulnerable foster youth and how a program like the one the news featured would have been so beneficial to me when I was in foster care in New York City. Then I looked up the contact information for the nonprofit online. I hadn't even heard of the organization before I read the article, but I felt really moved in my spirit to reach out to them.

I ended up sending an email to the Executive Director (ED) of Court Appointed Special Advocates (CASA)-NYC, letting her know that I really appreciated the work of the organization and the volunteers and that I didn't have any type of support like that when I was in care, but I wished I had. I let her know I had reached out to the Mayor's office and hoped it would help them keep their funding. The ED sent me an email reply a few days later, thanking me for my support. A few weeks after that, I happily read another news article about the organization. It highlighted that the administration had a change of heart and decided not to cut the funding to CASA-NYC for the upcoming year. I was certain that my outreach wasn't the deciding factor in getting the powers that be to change their mind, but I felt a tinge of pride for not staying silent when I had the opportunity to speak up. It was the first time I had ever shared my story to try to help other youth still in care, and it made me feel good to think that it had made even a minute difference.

With that good feeling filed in the back of my brain I went on about my life, trying to get my startup off the ground and managing all the stress that went along with it. It was a few months later when I was responding to customer inquiries that I came across an email from a film director. She said she had gotten my information from CASA-NYC—I assumed it was through the Executive Director. The director, Yasmin Mistry, was a court appointed special advocate (CASA) and had volunteered on a few youth cases. She wanted to help change the narrative about the youth in the child welfare system by doing an animated documentary on foster care that allowed former youth who were in foster care to share in their own words what the experience was like. Yasmin wanted to know if I was interested in sharing my story as one of the participants in her movie.

The request caught me off guard. Up until I felt compelled to try to help CASA-NYC by writing to the Mayor's office, I really hadn't considered sharing my story with anyone. The only other time I'd even mentioned that I had been in foster care was in a trusting moment early on in my career—and my boss had treated me differently ever since. Trepidation was all I felt as I thought about all the bad things that could happen if I were to publicly share my story. But that feeling drifted away as I thought about how good I felt after sharing my story to help the foster youth that CASA-NYC supported. And I felt pretty secure in the professional reputation that I had built, so I wasn't as concerned as I'd once been about being unfairly penalized for having been in foster care.

I was leaning towards saying yes, but I was a little worried about the director, Yasmin. I had lived long enough to know that just because someone claimed to have good intentions didn't mean they did. I wanted to know that she wouldn't twist my words and really wanted to help youth in care. I emailed her and we set up a time to meet and discuss the vision for her film. On the edge of where Soho meets the West Village in Manhattan, we met up a few weeks later early in the evening for a coffee chat at a trendy shop. It must have been late fall because I remember there was a slight chill in the air as I walked over from the co-working office in Tribeca.

Yasmin looked every bit the part of a NYC film director with the exception of her smile. It was too bright. Too warm. It gave off the hopeful vibes of someone with drive who hadn't let life compromise her big dreams. Almost immediately, I knew she would make her film a reality through sheer will. But if I was going to be in it, what I needed to know was *why*.

The answer revealed itself over the course of our conversation. Yasmin had volunteered for CASA for a few years and was frustrated that she had a bigger say in the lives of youth in care than they did. Film was her passion, and she really wanted to use the medium she loved to give kids in foster care a platform to tell their own stories in their own words. Yasmin had put out a call through her personal network and was hoping to get a few additional former foster care youth to participate in the animated documentary. She felt using animation was a creative way to visually convey the emotions and journey of youth sharing their story to the audience.

She also shared that she loved volunteering for CASA and being able to help youth and families. Because of her sporadic work hours, a lot of her current volunteering time was being spent doing ICPC paperwork. ICPC, the Interstate Compact on the Placement of Children, is the law that limits the movement of children across state lines in an attempt to prevent child trafficking. In order for foster youth to be placed with family across state lines, a lot of paperwork must be submitted to various government agencies. The process is long and tedious and can last from a few weeks or months up to a year in the most backlogged states; all the while, a child is waiting in limbo until everything is approved. I'd come to learn in subsequent years that doing ICPCs is a pretty dreaded part of the work for child welfare workers and volunteers. That's partly because of the laborious requirements, but more so because the waiting and being unable to know when the process will be complete is frustrating to everyone involved.

Everything Yasmin told me felt heartfelt and truthful but as I listened, I was still searching for the "why" in her answer. But then she segued, unconsciously, I think, to telling me about a youth case she had been assigned. Her eyes lowered to match the dropped register of her voice. I swore I saw her body tense. Leaning in, I watched the pain wash over her as she talked broadly about the "tragedy." She didn't divulge any specifics about the case, but I could see she was crushed. I couldn't be certain, but the pain etched on her face and her gentle, almost disbelieving tone as she spoke gave it away.

Every few years, there's a child welfare case that bubbles up in the news because the details are so horrific and so heartbreaking that the wall of indifference and complacency begins to crack, and society is forced to confront its failings head-on. People are reminded that there are children in care who are innocent and afraid, deserving of love and protection, who the system will fail. It's usually the death of a young child already in foster care or one where warning signs were ignored that inspires passionate, loud calls for reform—at least for a few months. Then the child's name fades from public consciousness and the urge for change wanes, until a few years later when the death of another child who the system failed to protect reignites the cycle again. Yasmin didn't need to reveal the depth of her "why." I already knew it. She was tired. Tired of the cycle and tired of feeling helpless within a broken system, so she wanted to try a new approach to change it. That was her "why." Or maybe it was mine.

We left the coffee shop about an hour later, saying our goodbyes before we walked out to the darkness that comes way too soon in the fall evening, with me fully committed to the film project and Yasmin's vision. It would be a few months of email updates before she had everything ironed out to begin shooting, but soon enough I found myself walking the Upper West Side to a hostel that Yasmin had booked which had a large, old, wood-adorned theater inside.

The emotional shoot lasted much of the day, with my face becoming tearstained several times as I answered Yasmin's questions about my time in care. Events that I hadn't thought about in years jumped to the front of my mind, with me recalling details as if I were living them again. All the feelings—fear, sadness, guilt, and anger—came rushing back as I relived the story of my youth. But so did the feelings of pride, incredulity, and hope as I shared the moments of resilience and strength that had carried me through those challenging times. With empathic eyes, Yasmin listened intently as she encouraged me to keep sharing. As I spoke, I realized that revisiting these memories was not just about reliving the past but also about acknowledging the journey I had undertaken. It was a fully cathartic experience, one that allowed me to come to terms with my past and give power to the growth and transformation that I had undergone since those difficult days.

After we wrapped, I felt emotionally lighter. It wasn't just that I had unburdened myself from the weight I had been carrying for so long, but that I had consciously chosen to take control of that weight, my pain, and my story, and tried to use it for good.

Over the next few months, I'd meet up with Yasmin and her film crew a few more times. She captured B-roll of me for the film at some of the elementary schools I attended, walking around some of my old Harlem neighborhoods and in front of my great-grandmother's building. Apparently, way more foster youth than she had expected had reached out to her, wanting to share their own foster care stories. So, she decided to make the documentary a series of films instead. Her first film would be my story, and she wanted to make sure she had enough atmospheric content of me to include in it.

Then, a few weeks before the film was complete, I experienced one of the most poignant moments of my life. Yasmin had set up a preview screening of a few clips of the film for a group of family court judges and social workers in the Bronx and wanted me there for the Q&A that would follow. As I walked up to the concrete building, the letters carved into the facade caught me by surprise. As I stared up at the words "FAMILY COURT," screaming at me in all caps, the realization hit me that I'd been here before. I'd already walked through these glass doors trimmed in black, through the tall metal detectors with their accusatory beeps, and down the fluorescent-lit corridors. I'd sat on the wood benches that lie right outside the cavernous courtrooms.

So much of my childhood was decided in this very building: in those courtrooms that I wasn't allowed access to, by adults who never bothered to ask what I needed or wanted. And now, by fate or destiny or by my own self-actualization, I found myself standing on the other side of those imposing doors, no longer a powerless child, but a young adult ready to make a difference.

The weight of the past and the potential for the future collided within me as I stepped into that familiar, formally intimidating space. It was as if the universe had conspired to bring me back to this very spot, but this time, I had a voice, a purpose, and the opportunity to advocate for those who, like my younger self, had been silenced and overlooked.

After the film played, I fielded questions from the judges and social workers in a conference room on a floor above the courtrooms. The room was filled with optimism, and the judges and social workers seemed to recognize the sincerity in my voice. Each question they posed was a reminder of the countless times I had yearned for someone to ask me what I needed or wanted as a child. I wasn't going to waste the chance to answer those questions, not just for myself, but for others in similar circumstances. As the questions continued, I confidently responded with clarity and passion, trying to ensure my words were filled with emotional impact to connect with my audience.

A few weeks letter it was the premiere night of *Feeling Wanted*. In Brooklyn, I found myself at an event space decorated with twinkling lights—and full of nerves. Yasmin had sent me an edit of the documentary to review, and I thought it turned out great. But I was still worried about how other people would respond to my story. Yasmin said a few words and briefly introduced me to the audience, with the announcement that they would be able to ask me questions after the film. Watching myself on the large screen was anxiety-inducing, but I was calmed by the emotional energy in the room. I could feel and see the audience leaning in—the soft sniffles, the head nods, the unexpected laughter. I felt them join me on the journey, be touched by my struggles, and collectively root for me to win.

To loud applause, I stood and moved to the front of the room to answer questions. I told them they could ask me anything and I would answer honestly. The room did not disappoint. They asked about how I felt now that I was years removed from foster care: *relieved but frustrated that youth in care were still experiencing the same trauma*. They asked what got me through when things were darkest: *knowing that my great-grandmother loved me*. They asked what I thought would make the child welfare system better: *burning it down and starting over. But short of that, stop punishing families for being poor and taking away their kids. Too many youth are taken away from their families not because they are being abused but because their parents lack resources and access.* And they asked how they could help.

This has become one of my favorite questions to answer over the years, and I've learned to tweak my response based on the audience I'm addressing. But the heart of my response has remained consistent since the first time the question was posed to me on premiere night: *Speak up and out about all the misconceptions of foster care, especially the idea that the children themselves have done anything wrong to be removed from their home or deserve what happens to them. No youth anywhere deserves to feel traumatized, afraid, abused, abandoned, or alone.*

Those initial screenings opened doors to other opportunities to raise awareness about the needs of youth in foster care. I realized that my journey in life had come full circle, and that everything I'd done, survived, and overcome had led me right here to the person I was supposed to be. I'd not only found my purpose, but I also saw that life had outfitted me with all the skills I needed to advocate for change in a meaningful way. My years in foster care gave me the lived experience to understand the unique challenges and the emotional toll that come with being a part of the foster care system and its aftermath. My years of traveling across the country and around the world, as well as my work in marketing, gave me the tools to tell my story in a real way, compelling others to lean in and care about the welfare of foster youth. My problems, my baggage, and my successes in spite of my struggles had made me the ideal messenger for this critical work.

In the years that followed, I evolved into a more vocal champion for youth in care, integrating my activism into the fabric of my life.

I became deliberate in ensuring that the media companies I aligned with supported my advocacy and my quest for a purpose-driven professional journey. It wasn't necessary for my colleagues to be fervent advocates for foster care youth themselves, but rather for them to be part of an environment that nurtured meaningful contributions to the community.

As I began to openly share my personal experiences, I discovered that my professional career thrived even more. It wasn't because I made foster care the only aspect of my life I leaned into, but because I simply embraced my "baggage" as an essential part of who I am. I stopped hiding the parts of me that made me authentically myself. And as it turns out, my bosses, co-workers, and clients seemed even more excited to work with me, listen to my recommendations, and sometimes even support my advocacy efforts. In both my work and personal life, they recognized me as someone who had confronted adversity, learned invaluable life lessons, and exhibited unwavering resilience in the face of challenges. If I could survive foster care, juggle being a national advocate with my side fashion and lifestyle TV work, and thoroughly love life as much as I do, then I could rally a team to come up with creative marketing ideas and get a national campaign out the door on time and on budget. Being good with who I was unshackled me to be the best at what I did, and that made me a desirable employee, collaborator, leader, and influencer in my field.

It also made me a source of inspiration and motivation for others, encouraging them to embrace their own uniqueness and reach their fullest potential. Child welfare organizations invited me to give keynote speeches and share my story to help attract more volunteers and foster or adoptive parents, or to help them raise funds to provide resources to youth in care. The organization, CASA-NYC, which had inspired me to speak out on behalf of foster care youth for the first time, invited me to join its board. I was hesitant at first since I assumed that people on charity boards needed to have deep pockets to make donations, which I was unable to do. They shared that having someone outspoken with lived experience as a foster care youth on their board was of more importance to them. I was really impressed by the work that they did with their volunteers, so I gladly joined to help them in their goals to increase the number of youth in New York City assigned a CASA volunteer. I also joined the board of City Living NY, a nonprofit dedicated to helping youth who have aged out of care avoid homelessness and gain independence and self-sufficiency.

On my social media platforms, I became a resource to help educate anyone who wanted to learn about foster care through an "Ask Me Anything" series of video posts where I answer questions posed to me by my followers or people who contact me. In truth, I answer questions about any topic that I'm knowledgeable about—how to find a mentor, what clothing styles are trending, how to become comfortable with public speaking—but the majority of the questions posed from my audience are on the topic of foster care. I like being a safe space on the internet where people can get a perspective from someone who has lived experience as they continue to learn about ways they can help youth in care. And I like knowing that I'm having a real impact on inspiring people to take action—for themselves and for others.

I've had a few moments along the way that affirmed my decision to stop checking my baggage at the door and show up as the best version of me. One happened early on and followed a *Feeling Wanted* screening. Yasmin texted me about a week after to tell me that one of the event attendees—a former foster care youth—had emailed her to say that he decided to enroll in college after hearing me speak. That moment still gives me chills. Another moment happened during a screening in Westchester County, NY. After the film played and Yasmin and I had wrapped the Q&A session, the County Executive surprised us both by designating May 19 as Charell Star and Yasmin Mistry Day in Westchester County. The honor was humbling, but what stood out to me most about that day was a woman in the audience. As I stood during the presentation, she caught my eye. I couldn't place her, but she felt so familiar, and she had a cute little infant in a carrier on her chest. After the formal event wrapped, we got the chance to chat, and it turned out she and I met at a *Feeling Wanted* screening a year earlier. She had been inspired by the film and my words to become a foster parent. The baby she'd brought with her to the event was her first placement.

A slightly humorous moment came in the form of an ad that popped up in my feed while I was mindlessly scrolling Instagram.

I stopped mid-scroll because I saw myself ugly crying in the video. Apparently, Yasmin had cut some of the extra unused documentary footage into promotional clips for the film. This clip that caught me by surprise featured me talking about how dehumanizing it feels as a child who is being torn from everything they know to then have their personal items thrown into a trash bag.

A nonprofit that provides free luggage to foster care youth had used the clip to bring attention to the fact that this is still how many youth in foster care are moved through the system. Every day a kid is made to feel like trash simply because the expediency of moving that child into foster care had been placed above having empathy for that child. Watching the video filled me with so much pride. Not only were my words being used to bring awareness to the issue, but they were being used by an organization to create meaningful change.

One of the biggest moments yet that has reinforced in me that shrinking parts of myself is a disservice was the interview I did with Brandon Stanton for his extremely popular photoblog, "Humans of New York." Stanton usually interviewed people at random on the streets of New York, but with the pandemic raging and people on the streets far and few between, he started selecting subjects based on recommendations. Someone recommended me to him, and so I found myself outside his apartment building in Manhattan waiting nervously for him to appear. He did, a few minutes after I arrived, and we ended up walking to a nearby courtyard a few blocks away that was just quiet enough to make you forget we were in the heart of New York City.

It was two or three hours later that we said our goodbyes after an emotional—and at times teary—interview where I answered a stream of questions about my life, time in foster care, love of fashion, and recovering fear of dogs. He had taken photos throughout the interview and since I'm an ugly crier, I worried some might be less than flattering. A few weeks later we did a Zoom follow-up interview that lasted a few hours and then met up in the city again a few weeks after that. About a month later, he emailed me to let me know he was going to post my story on Instagram, Facebook, and his blog the next day. He prepped me that the response to the story might be "overwhelming" but that his community "would hold me tight."

He was right on both accounts. Humans of New York has more than 29 million followers on its Instagram and Facebook accounts alone. That doesn't even include the number of readers on the Humans of NY blog or sites that re-blog his posts. It was the largest audience that I had ever opened myself up to and shared my story with.

In the end, my story helped raise more than $140,000 for CASA-NYC, and people from across the country messaged me to let me know they had signed up to volunteer as a CASA advocate. What's more, I received so many messages from former and current foster care youth, who thanked me for trying to help and shared their own stories of adversity with me. Some of those stories were hard to read and I had to talk with my therapist about the right ways to process the pain that so many of the youth were dealing with. But I was humbled by the fact that they finally had someone who they felt safe enough to share with, and I tried to give them support wherever I could. It took me about a year to respond to all the emails, DMs, and other messages I received, but it was one of the most profound experiences that I've ever had.

Sharing my story with the world—whether through the documentary *Feeling Wanted,* speaking engagements, or my interview with Humans of New York—allowed me to connect with people on a profound level, opened doors, and created opportunities I couldn't have imagined during my early career. I've come to realize that being true to myself and embracing my past doesn't hinder my success; it amplifies it. As I look back on my journey, I'm so glad that I stopped trying to "check my baggage at the door" and instead learned that baggage—good, bad, and otherwise—is part of how I travel, how I fly.

CHAPTER 19
The Legacy Remains

My aunt Merlé was hardly what I'd call a soft person. My earliest memories of her were watching her ball at "The Cage," a basketball court on West 4th Street in Manhattan. There are a few courts in New York City that you do not step foot on unless you are absolutely confident that your level of game play rivals that of players in the starting lineup of the NBA, and "The Cage" is one of them.

After we were reunified, my mom would bring my sister and me to watch my aunt play on the weekends from time to time, and I'd restlessly stare through the chain-link fence as she not only held her own but humbled quite a few players whose size or sex foolishly led them to believe they could guard her. It was all fun and games until she got that ball in her hands, and she would, most definitely, get that ball in her hands. I'm pretty sure if she had been born a generation later, she would have played in the WNBA; she was just that good. But as it happens, she had no say over when she was born. So, she played street ball and continued for a couple of years in college.

Merlé was actually the first member of my family to attend college. I'd beat her to the graduation stage, but she'd best me in the end—earning not only her bachelor's but also master's and doctorate degrees. She also proudly served in the Navy sometime after her first go at college, and the framed photo of her in her military uniform was the only one I ever saw of her in a skirt. White tanks and long basketball shorts were Merlé's preferred attire, but she also had a pretty cool sense of individual style, rocking oversized suits on her towering frame or sweater vests over white tees coordinated with baggy jeans and kicks. She was aware that her bold lack of conformity to feminist ideals made her stand out and was comfortable with that. Looking at her, you would assume instantly that she gave zero f*cks about what people thought of her. But you'd be wrong.

Even as a kid I knew that being liked was important to Merlé. Always quick to break the tension by cracking a joke or pushing herself beyond her means to help, she repeatedly would take on others' issues in the hopes of simply being accepted. Sometime this saviorism would be really beneficial, like the time when she let my mom, my sister, and me live with her. We'd been reunified with my mom for a few months, and the small one-bedroom apartment that we were living in became overrun with mice. I'd stayed in apartments with mice before and although they made me uneasy—scampering around corners late with their giant eyes—I never knew I was supposed to be afraid of them until the first time I heard my mother's piercing scream at the sight of one. Core memory locked. The next day, she met me at school with my sister in tow and we took the train to my aunt's house, where we stayed for a few months until the building super confirmed with my mother that the apartment was mouse-free.

While we stayed with my aunt, crammed into her one-bedroom apartment, it was clear—from the jokes and stories they reminisced about—that she and my mom loved each other. Yet I could also sense an underlying strain between them, a tension I would only begin to understand as I grew older and started to confront my own sources of trauma. As a child, this awkwardness simply lingered, unresolved and confusing. Despite this, Merlé made an effort to negotiate the peace in other ways. A few days after we moved in with her, she sat me down and encouraged me to give my mom a chance, sensing my discomfort of living with my mom and reassuring me that my mom was "trying hard."

Merlé tended to dole out forgiveness easily—perhaps too easily—and for a long time, it seemed she equated forgiveness with healing.

She was mistaken in this belief, but her intention was genuine. At the time, she was the only adult who even acknowledged my feelings, and for that reason, I appreciated her and felt a strong connection to her.

I wasn't the only one. Merlé had a knack for connecting with all types of people. She could go from stranger to bestie with anyone—movie stars, award-winning musicians, the homeless person on the street. There were no airs around her and that made it so easy to get along with her. She'd go from working as a bouncer in the hottest nightclubs in the city to doing personal security for A-listers like Jay-Z, Busta Rhymes, Mark Wahlberg, Missy Elliott, DMX, and Aaliyah—who all liked to be around her. She then parlayed her entertainment connections into a full-time role as the music manager for the daytime talk show, *The Queen Latifah Show*.

With her career change into television, she took it upon herself to open a door for me. Her show had openings for paid summer interns/ushers, and she got me hired as one. As a rising college freshman, I found myself to be the youngest intern on the staff. All the other interns were at least juniors in college. I was so green that when a curious audience member asked how I got the job, I answered honestly, "Oh, my aunt works here." My boss overheard and told me not to say that again.

I hadn't thought anything of it since my aunt introduced me as her niece to everyone on the staff, but apparently, you're not supposed to admit that a family member helped you land a job. I was too new to the corporate world to understand nepotism and Merlé was too excited by being able to help me out to care. Regardless, I really enjoyed my summer of working on the show and impressed my bosses enough to be able to pick up some extra work assisting the booking and publicity department. And it was the first time I got to see Merlé in her element.

She was all smiling every time I'd run into her in the office—we were on different office floors, so I didn't see her most days. When I did see her, she was always happily buzzing, coming from or going to a meeting or running to take a call. I had known from her music collection that she was really into music; I hadn't realized that jobs like music managers for TV shows existed. Of course, someone would need to license music for the show and work with the artist management teams for bookings, but I didn't know there was a singular person responsible for it or how any of it actually happened until my aunt exposed me to it. It was a pretty cool job, and she seemed to genuinely love it.

Unfortunately, the show was canceled after two seasons, but Merlé was excited to share big news with me during one of my college breaks: she was producing and co-hosting a lifestyle show for Oxygen titled *She-Commerce*. The show focused on the trending news and fashion of the day. I congratulated her and told her she had the coolest job ever. I'd seen tons of people on TV talking about fashion but never knew you could make a job out of it. And, although my aunt had an awesome sense of personal style, I had no idea that she was even that into fashion. She was honestly the only person I knew who wasn't all talk, and who actively manifested her dreams into reality.

Months later, after her show ended—it didn't get renewed for a second season—Merlé called me excitedly while I was heading back to my dorm from class. She had just finished writing a book and wanted to tell me about it. Happy for her, I listened as she spilled all the details. It was a memoir and told the story of her life: surviving sexual abuse at the hands of a family member, recovering from drug abuse, uncovering repressed trauma, how she was infected with HIV—and how it changed her life. I'd known about her HIV diagnosis since I was in high school—because of my grandmother's weaponization of the info—but my aunt had never said the words to me herself. Until that moment, it was something left unsaid between the two of us, but she decided to open up to me and to the world with her book. I told her I was proud of her for writing the book and was excited to read it. A few days later a copy arrived at my dorm.

Foolishly, I had thought that when my aunt said the book was finished, she meant she had a draft or manuscript printouts from Microsoft Word. Instead, I was holding a fully self-published softcover book with an ISBN number ready to be sold. Titled *Getting Unstuck: Girl to Girl You Can Be Infected Indeed,* the memoir was direct, raw, and an honest portrayal of the brutal life she survived and how she made it through. Unable to put it down, I finished reading it in two days. Instead of shock or disbelief, the words left me with a strong sense of relief. Even before I was reunified with my mom, adults around me had told me that family business was private business and "what happens in the house, stays in the house." Even if you were being harmed by the secrets they kept, I was taught there was no bigger betrayal than inviting scrutiny. And, with 260 pages of her words, my aunt set that lie ablaze.

Admiration is what I felt for Merlé and even more so when she clarified the author's name she'd chosen to list on her book: "Conscious." "I was asleep for so long and these memories awakened me," she told me. "Conscious" wasn't just a pen name but one that represented who she was now, so she started introducing herself with that name. She told me I could continue to call her "Merlé," though, I think because she wasn't quite ready to fully let go of that part of herself. During summer break, on some of my days off from work, I'd tag along with her to book signings at local bookstores in Brooklyn and Harlem and help her sell copies at community festivals. She could get anyone who stopped at the table to buy a book.

Enthralled and equally proud of her after hearing her summarize what the book was about, customers were instantly transformed into her personal fans, promising to tell their friends about the book as well. Using my limited public relations knowhow—I was still learning in college—I wrote a press release for the book and would accompany Merlé to media interviews from time to time. The coolest one, for us both, was the interview she landed on the New York City radio station Hot 97. These days radio stations may feel like a relic medium from decades gone by, but growing up Hot 97 was probably the best-known station in New York City—and they had invited Merlé for an interview and she wanted me to be there to see it.

Composed, bright, funny, she nailed the interview and gave off no indications that she was even the least bit anxious about it all. Not until we were driving back to her house in NJ and her car ran out of gas in the Holland Tunnel did she let on. As the police officer walked up to her window, she blurted out with a laugh, "Officer, sir, I was just on the radio and was so nervous I forgot to get gas beforehand." Luckily a yellow cab driver was right behind us, and with her car in neutral, he was nice enough to push us in front of his car to a station right outside the tunnel on the NJ side.

Not too long after, Merlé bought a house and moved to Miami, Florida. She wanted to chase her dreams in the sun and put some distance between her and family ties holding her back. She'd call me with updates on her life semi-regularly and I'd see her whenever she came back to NYC for work or visits. Continuing to reinvent herself, she was excited to share the news that she turned her memoir into a one-woman show. She was playing the lead and was taking acting classes in Miami. Never one to under-deliver on her projects, she lined up a multi-city tour for the show and I brought roses to her off-Broadway debut. It was during the time I was running my startup, and she hired one of my personal assistants to staff her book table sales after the show. The line was so long that I ended up helping out with the sales too.

Around this time, I noticed that the tone of our catchup calls started to change. Whereas in the past, it was really Merlé dishing on what was new in her life, now she would ask my thoughts on the updates. A lot of times, I would be happily offering her positive encouragement or advice on her latest project, but sometimes I was forced to share a more sober outlook.

Like one time when Merlé recapped a call she had with her mother—my grandmother. She refused a financial request—I honestly can't remember the amount—and my grandmother apparently responded by cussing her out and refusing to talk to her. Instead, my grandmother had been spending time talking with my mom, and it was really grating on my aunt that she was being ignored. "Can you believe that she's being childish and won't talk to me?" my aunt asked. I tended to refrain from weighing in on my grandmother's antics, but this time I responded.

"Yes," I replied. "This happens every six months. She can't get her way with one of you, so she makes the other one her favorite. I've watched her do this my entire life."

"Wow," she said like an epiphany hit her. "You really recognized that?"

"Yes," I said again. "She plays you two against each other and makes you fight each other for her love. You've got to see the pattern."

"You right. That's crazy that you noticed that," Merlé chimed in. At first, I thought she might be patronizing me, but there was a long pause after her words. As she gathered herself, it dawned on me that she hadn't seen the pattern after all the years of being used, then pitted against her sister—even though it happened regularly. And then I realized the reason she couldn't see it was that she was too wrapped up in it. It's no secret to me that my aunt and my mom wanted nothing more than to be loved by their own mother and that, instead of returning that love, she exploited it time and time again. Regardless of what she did or how many times she did it, Merlé and my mom always let her back in their life because they just wanted her to love them. As Merlé and I continued talking, I could tell the conversation had rattled her a bit, but she agreed to bring it up with her therapist the next time they met and by the end of the call she was back to cracking jokes and sharing her upcoming project plans.

By this time, Merlé had relocated to Los Angeles and was focused on getting her book made into a movie. She ended up taking a job to help offset the cost of self-funding her movie, but being Merlé it wasn't just any job. She networked her way into being the tutor for an A-list celebrity's kids who were really struggling in school. It was definitely an out-of-the-box career choice for her, but she was incredibly smart. If anyone could help those kids understand their schoolwork, she could. Her job was going well, and the kids went from questionable grades to getting high marks in their classes. She called after my morning spin class to tell me some good news.

"Guess what," she whispered so low, I could barely hear her.

"Why are you whispering? Who are you hiding from?" I asked.

Laughing, Merlé said, "I just got a raise, and I don't want anyone to know." She had done such a good job helping her charges raise their grades that she was able to convince her boss to pay her a lot more for her efforts.

"That's great," I replied back in a normal voice. "You should get a financial advisor and make sure to invest some of it," I continued. "Oh and…" I started to say, but she cut me off with "I know." I laughed when she did.

My aunt wasn't great with money. Like many people trying to

break generational curses, she never wanted to be perceived as poor, so that meant buying the things she couldn't have when she had nothing. She'd send me pictures of her white drop-top and would tell me how much things cost in her house. Even with her disposable spending, I figured that much of her money went to funding her movie. I was shocked when she confided in me that she was getting stressed out about the amount of money she was sending family members. Even before the raise it sounded like they were bleeding her dry, and she was constantly saying "yes" because she felt guilty saying "no."

I was pretty sure she was telling me about her raise and financial woes with our family because she knew I made decent money as well and also knew I had stopped funding my family's foolishness years ago. I told her that she needed to start telling people "no" when they called her with sob stories, and that she was never going to get ahead on her projects if she was funding the lifestyles of able-bodied adults. I recommended she change her phone number, but she was worried that would be a problem if her clients suddenly couldn't get hold of her. A few weeks later she texted me to tell me that she had started telling people "no" and was blocking the numbers of people who weren't taking "no" for an answer. She admitted it was emotionally hard for her, but she seemed to be following through, and I was proud of her for setting her boundaries and sticking to them.

As Merlé was tightening her circle, her tutoring business appeared to be on the cusp of expanding. She called to tell me that two other A-listers had heard about her educational prowess and were interested in hiring her to help their kids as well. We brainstormed some ways she could grow her company quickly if she landed the new clients, like hiring local college students majoring in math and science and training them in her method of tutoring. She liked the idea and worked hard on a proposal for her services.

Although things were going well for her, I had concerns. When I saw her on a work trip I took to LA, she was so impulsive and wild in her demeanor that it was obvious she was using drugs again. I confirmed as much with my god-sister who also lives in LA and saw Merlé more frequently than I did.

Merlé had also started to act more transactional in our

communications during this time. She used to ask questions about how I was doing or what I was working on, but that happened less and less frequently so that the conversations were mainly me listening to her and then giving her advice. And one time when she needed help with a question on her tutoring expansion proposal, she texted me, "I will take care of you financially." That rubbed me the wrong way, and I brought it up to her when we connected. I always assumed one of the things that my aunt liked about our relationship was that I never asked her for money. I was helping her—brainstorming business ideas, writing press releases, attending her events, supporting her endeavors—because I truly loved her and wanted her to succeed.

And I felt she had helped me for the same reason—from getting me that internship on the TV show to coming to my college graduation to letting me print out like a hundred resumes on her home printer when I was looking for my first post-college PR job. Money wasn't a factor in our relationship, and I knew it was important to both of us that it never was. She apologized when I called her out on her funky Hollywood-esque text, and I forgave her for it, but she was still far from being her old self whenever we connected.

As it turned out, I wouldn't get to see that vibrant version of my aunt again. During a tutoring session she made a transgression in scolding one of the A-lister's kids when they did something they weren't supposed to be doing. She ended up getting fired and her hopes for expanding her business were dashed. It absolutely crushed her to know that people she believed liked and respected her—and who it was clear she had come to care about—could disregard her so easily. She spiraled downward after that, and the few times we talked it was clear that she was high.

The very last time she and I spoke, she asked me to loan her $10,000. It was the same amount my best friend had lent me when I wanted to buy my condo, so the number held spiritual significance for me. She said she needed it for her car and some bills, but I didn't feel comfortable giving her the money in her state. I had been around people in the throes of addiction my entire life and I knew everything professionals say against enabling their lifestyle. I wanted my aunt to get better, so I did what I was supposed to do in that situation.

However, knowing that didn't alleviate the guilt I felt when I got the call telling me she'd passed away.

Was I her last lifeline? Did she feel abandoned by the one person she thought she could count on? Could I have helped?

The official examiner's report listed "overdose" as the cause of death, but that's just the abbreviated version of the truth. My aunt had battled substance abuse for decades, but it was a direct outcome of her attempt to self-medicate the pain of the childhood trauma she experienced and the betrayal of those who were supposed to hold her close. What killed her was the weight of the jagged pieces of her broken heart that pulled her down one more time than she could get back up. Before now, she'd always gotten back up. Merlé fought her way back from the brink more times than I can count and probably even more times than I'm aware of. But this last heartbreak pulled her under before she could see her way out.

It took every ounce of strength I had to look in her casket and the moment I did, I instantly regretted it. The pale, shriveled figure that lay in that box looked nothing like the woman I remembered. And that hurt my soul. But the funeral home was filled with people whose words and stories brought her true profile back to life. They talked about her big dreams and even bigger drive to make them real. They shared stories of how she'd make them laugh and bring them out of darkness. They reminisced about their first meetings and how that moment changed their lives. And they spoke about how her death wasn't what she left behind—her light was. Their words were warm and calming because they were true.

In the time I got to spend with her, Merlé taught me so much about life just by being herself. One of the biggest lessons was that the world doesn't get to put you in a box. Reinvention is a form of growth, and you shouldn't be afraid of your own evolution. Just dream as big as you're willing to strive.

Another profound lesson I learned from observing her was the importance of understanding what you need to be your best self. Merlé sought to be accepted for who she was, and there's nothing wrong with that. It's what we all desire at our core. When she realized that her family's support wasn't fulfilling her needs, she ventured out and created a new circle of people who made her feel seen and inspired her to grow. Those were the people who filled her funeral hall, and those are the people who continue to carry her memory. It wasn't just about the life she lived but about the bold lives she encouraged others to embrace. That is her enduring legacy.

She left this world, but not before staking her claim within it and showing everyone she met that it was their right to do the same.

CHAPTER 20
Good People Are Kind

MY LIFE HAS been negatively impacted by so many awful humans that it comes as a surprise to many—me included, sometimes—that I haven't given up on people altogether. That's because, for all the negative individuals I've encountered, I've been blessed to meet unbelievably wonderful individuals who not only restored my faith in humanity but held space for me to heal, grow, and love. I don't know where I'd be without their support and the light they brought into my life.

There were teachers and advisors who became my saviors, showing me that strangers can care about and want to help for no other reason than having a kind heart. There were girlfriends who became my sisters, proving that family is the people who you choose and those who choose you. There were colleagues turned mentors who showed me that relationships built on mutual respect and shared aspirations could lead to not only professional fulfillment but also genuine camaraderie. And there was my GG, who showed me that unconditional love was possible. However, it was the man who would become my husband who made me so aware of the power of this type of love that it made me sad for people—especially the ones who tried to hurt me—who I knew would never experience it.

I was in my early 30s, and I met Stephen as people often do these days—on an online dating site. Our initial direct messages were pretty formal, more so on my end than his, as I tend to keep my digital conversations exactingly professional with people I don't know. That formality stayed consistent for a few direct messages back and forth until we started talking about some of our favorite TV shows. One of the shows he mentioned that he really enjoyed was one I was exceedingly obsessed with at the time: *Rome*. I'm quite sure I wrote him a long and impassioned email on why I considered it one of the best series ever, and he replied wittily that he agreed. It was nice to connect with someone in a real way even though we were engaging through screens.

Our emails to each other became more frequent, and a few weeks later we met up for our first date at a small restaurant called Yerba Buena on Perry Steet in the West Village—his pick. I arrived before he did. It had been raining, so I went to the ladies' room to freshen up and then pulled up a stool at the bar to wait. For about 20 minutes, I sat sipping water and glancing at the door. Finally, I opened the dating app and went to our last direct message confirming our meeting time. He had included his cell phone number, so I texted him that I was at the restaurant sitting at the bar.

A stalking incident in college had made me leery of sharing my phone number with guys before I had gotten to know them, so I was a little annoyed at having to text him and reveal my phone number. Less than 10 seconds later, he rushed through the door, a little wet from the rain. He walked straight up to me at the bar to apologize. He had actually arrived but didn't see me inside (because I had been in the ladies' room), so he waited outside to greet me since it was raining, and this restaurant could be hard to spot. He was flustered and apologetic, and *ridiculously cute*.

Our dinner was fun, filled with effortless conversation. We chatted about everything from the state of education in America—he's an educator—to the best *Star Trek* series, "Next Generation," of course. We stayed so late that the restaurant started turning chairs upside down around us—an effective if unsubtle hint. The rain let up, so we decided to head to a bar after dinner to grab a drink. We found a cute one a few blocks away, posted up at the bar, laughed and chatted. He excused himself to go to the bathroom and while he was gone, the bartender asked me if this was our first date. I told him yes, and he replied, "He's nice. You should go out with him again." I gave a playful grin while filing his suggestion away and continued to sip on my cocktail.

Before we knew it, it was closing time at the bar. The rain had started up again, so we decided to share a taxi. Since he lived in New Jersey, we asked the driver to drop him off at the PATH train station first before heading to my stop in Queens. We continued to laugh and chat as the car glided through the brightly lit streets. When the car arrived at the station, we exchanged goodbyes, and Stephen handed the driver some cash before he hopped out of the car. I assumed he'd given him enough to cover his portion of the ride, but the driver purposefully caught my eyes in the rearview mirror. Staring intently, he asked, "Is this your first date with him?" Smiling, I responded, "Yes?"

"You should go out with him again. He's a nice guy," he replied as he pulled off to drive me home.

Around 30 minutes later, the driver stopped in front of my place. When I went to hand him cash for the ride, he refused it, saying in a kind tone, "Your date took care of it." To this day, I have no idea how much money Stephen overpaid for my ride home. But anyone who could turn skeptical New Yorkers into hopeless romantics, from the bartender to the taxi driver, was clearly someone special.

So, we went out again… and again and again. The more time I spent with Stephen, the more I fell in love with him. He was funny without ever being mean. He was passionate about his work as an educator and took pride in the stories he'd share about his students doing well on a test or a great essay they wrote for college. Stephen was equally accomplished and humble, downplaying his standing as a national expert in middle and high school literacy or that schools across the country requested him by name to come train their English teachers.

But it wasn't just humility: Stephen was determined to put others first, and not just his students. He loved his family deeply and went out of his way to make time for his friends. He gave to charity and believed in supporting his local community. The iron deficiency I'd come to learn I had that no one believed me about—Stephen did. He always believed me the first time I told him something. He was kind and thoughtful, sending me flowers just because or asking me how an event turned out that I had forgotten I had even mentioned to him weeks before. He was just an amazing and loving person, a *good* person. When I was with him, it made it hard to dwell on people who didn't measure up.

That's the thing about people who radiate kindness—you naturally gravitate to them. You want to not only be around that kindness but put the same type of energy into the world. Stephen was a former reporter, well aware of the injustices of the world. So, his general disposition of warmth—a choice he actively made—made it easy to see life through a softer lens, as if a smile and a kind word could be the keys to setting humanity right. It's not that his life was without struggle, but he consciously chose to navigate it with compassion and a willingness to be there for those who needed him. His brightness made me feel brighter, and his loving support helped me grow in ways I didn't know were possible.

It was Stephen's words that reaffirmed my decision to share my story in a foster care documentary and later become an advocate: "I'm proud of you." It was his whispers that calmed my fears when I was struggling to figure out a way to leave public relations and start a new career: "You deserve to be happy and work in a job you love." It was his encouragement that stood as a guiding light during the times I was frustrated at the amount of work I was doing but not getting paid for my TV segments: "You wanted to do that and made it happen. That's inspiring. See where it goes." His unwavering support wasn't just casual endorsements; it was a steady pillar that held me up when doubt crept in. His belief in my potential fueled my confidence, making all those moments feel like stepping stones toward something greater. He believed my voice mattered and my message was worth sharing. He made me believe it, too.

So, when he proposed, in the most thoughtful and romantic surprise trip to my favorite city in the world, Paris, I happily said, "Yes." Stephen was a good man, the type of man who has your back, and would be an amazing life partner and incredible friend. Saying yes to marrying him was a wholehearted affirmation of the life I knew we could build together—a lifetime filled with shared dreams, unwavering support, and a love that had already proven itself in both ordinary and extraordinary moments. In my yes was not only my love for him but my excitement for all the adventures, challenges, and joys that awaited us on our journey together.

We married on a boat on the Hudson River, floating between our home states of New York and New Jersey, surrounded by our family and friends. In our vows, we promised to love and cherish one another and support each other's dreams like they were our own. A few years later, like married couples do, we bought a house and moved to the suburbs with an eye to eventually raising kids. After a few years of growing, surviving, and enjoying life together, we met our son.

An email came from our adoption agency social worker, stating that they urgently needed to speak to us. On the call, they shared that a two-week-old baby boy—who happened to be born on Stephen's birthday—was in the NICU, and they wanted to know if we'd be interested in bringing him home. After some quick glances, we enthusiastically replied yes. Our social worker said, "Ok. Great, because his birth mom selected you to be his parents from your profile book."

The next day, donning facemasks and hospital gowns, our son was placed in my arms. Holding him, I felt scared, unsure of my abilities, and like a wave of emotions was about to overcome me—but then Stephen put his hands on my shoulders, his eyes smiling as he peered tenderly at this small ball of life in my arms. The room went quiet, my mind went still, and my heart tingled with fullness. Then Stephen said, loud enough to be heard over the cadre of machines beeping endlessly but soft enough that it was still a gentle whisper, "Hi Cole. We're your mom and dad." And, for the first time in my very long life, my eyes teared up—not from fear or trauma—but from an overwhelming surge of love and joy.

Stephen showed me that the most beautiful moments in life often come unexpectedly, in the midst of uncertainty and vulnerability. In that hospital room, as we silently expanded our hearts and vows to include our son, I looked out on the uncharted waters of motherhood and on our future together with boundless love for my husband, for my son, and for myself. Life is made up of moments: ones that hurt you, ones that heal you, ones that move you forward, and ones that are wrapped in love. And, in this moment, I felt healed, whole, and completely at home.

Acknowledgements

To everyone who has helped me along in this journey to becoming the person I smile at when I stand in the mirror—this book is a reflection not just of my experiences but of the love, wisdom, and encouragement each of you has shared. As I look back, I am overwhelmed with gratitude for the countless ways my tribe has influenced my life. The courage to write this book could not have come to life without the support, inspiration, and grounding that you have all provided.

To my incredible husband, Stephen Chiger—thank you for your unwavering love and support and for always protecting my dreams as if they were your own. Your belief in me has been my constant anchor, and I'm grateful every day that I get to walk this journey with you.

To my sweet son, CL—I'm so proud to be your mom. You amaze me every day, and watching you grow fills me with hope and wonder. You inspire me to be my best self.

To my Great Grandmother—thank you for caring for me when I needed it most. Your love and warmth gave me a foundation I could always rely on, and I am forever grateful for the strength you instilled in me.

To my Mom—thank you for showing me what not giving up looks like. I'm in awe of how far you've come and all you've accomplished. You inspire me, and I love you.

To Schnell Johnson, my forever BFF and my sister—we've been through so much together, and I am endlessly grateful for you. I'm in awe of the incredible mother, wife, and leader you are and how you make room in your heart for everyone in your life. In the moments when I doubt my faith, I remember that the only proof I need of a higher power is having you as my friend.

To Jessica Byers Larson—your love for life and the courage to seek out the fun in life is something I admire deeply, and I'm grateful for the warmth and openness you bring to every friendship, especially ours. Thank you for sharing that joy and for being a constant reminder of how much beauty there is to explore in this world.

To Kaitlyn Van Aalsburg—our friendship has grown so naturally from the day we met, and I'm so happy to see the wonderful life you've created. You're a fantastic mom and incredible professional, and you balance it all with such grace. Thank you for being a steady, supportive friend and inspiring me to be a little braver.

To Kayla Rose, my wonderful publicist—thank you for your endless enthusiasm, creativity, and dedication to sharing my story in the most authentic way possible. You're a force, and I can't wait to see the mark you leave on the world.

To Keyaira Boone—your joy for life is contagious, and I'm inspired by how hard you work to make your dreams reality. I can't wait to witness all the incredible things that lie ahead for you.

To Janelle Collins—I'm so thankful for our very funny first meeting and glad that I get to call you my friend. You have this incredible way of pouring love, humor, and light into the lives of those around you, and you make life better just by being in it. I'm endlessly grateful for you.

To Heather Richards—I am constantly amazed by how gracefully you juggle your roles as a brilliant professional and an incredible mom to three beautiful kids. Thank you for your kindness, your empathy, and the way you show up with such a full heart. I am so lucky to have you in my life.

To Wasidah Francois—thank you for being such a great friend and for always being there with support, encouragement, and a big heart. Your work as an entrepreneur and your passion for empowering women inspire me every day. I'm grateful for the way you lift others up, and I'm lucky to have you in my corner. You truly make the world a better place.

To LaToya Christian—you are such an amazing friend, peer, and role model. The way you inspire everyone around you to be better, including me, is something I truly admire. You exude strength, grace, and brilliance, and I'm so grateful to have you in my life. You push me to be my best, and I can't thank you enough for that.

To April Sawyer, my not so baby sister—thank you for giving me a reason to fight, to love, to endure. I'm so proud of the mom you've become and am so excited to see what your passion brings to the world.

To Andrew Sobel— thank you for always making me feel like part of the family. Your thoughtful feedback on the final round of my book meant so much, and I'm incredibly grateful for your support. You've always welcomed me with open arms, and I truly appreciate the way you've shown up for me, not just as my husband's best friend, but as a friend to me too. It means more than you know.

To Yasmin Mistry, my first director—thank you for igniting my passion for foster care advocacy and encouraging me to use my voice to make a difference. Your work has touched so many lives through your art, and I know you've only just begun. I'm forever grateful for your guidance and inspiration, and I strive every day to live up to the example you've set.

To Kerry Moles—thank you for your unwavering dedication to advocating for children and youth in foster care and ensuring their voices are heard. Your leadership and compassion inspire everyone around you, and I'm deeply grateful for the impact you make in the lives of children and young people every day. I often say that if I had a CASA, my experience in foster care might have been different, and if that CASA had been trained under your leadership, I know it would have been.

To Liz Northcutt— your passion and commitment to supporting young people as they transition out of foster care is truly inspiring. The work you do changes lives, and I'm in awe of your dedication to creating brighter futures. When youth in care ask me why they should risk opening their hearts after so many have let them down, I tell them it's because good people, like you, really do exist.

To Brandon Stanton—I was a fan of *Humans of New York* for years before our paths crossed and have always been inspired by your ability to tell stories with such authenticity and heart. I'm forever humbled that you not only shared mine but also amplified it to drive real change for youth in foster care. *HONY* isn't just your work; it's a legacy that reminds the world of our shared humanity and the power of storytelling. I'm grateful to be a small part of it and even more grateful to know you.

Xyana And Leilani Dewindt—thank you for being my amazing editors. Your recommendations and insights helped me refine my words and find my voice in a deeper, more meaningful way. This book is better because of you, and I am forever grateful for your expertise and support.

To Anna Bovi, my spectacular cover artist—thank you for turning my vision into something so breathtakingly real. Your artistry didn't just create a cover; it captured the brightness in my heart and how I choose to see the world.

Alaina Clark-Weinstein—thank you so much for generously sharing your publishing expertise with me and guiding me through this process. Your support and insights were invaluable in turning my manuscript into a published book, and I'm beyond grateful for your time, care, and wisdom.

To the teachers who showed me kindness and safety—thank you for providing a haven in those early days. You planted seeds of self-belief and made me feel valued in ways you may never know. And to my mentors, thank you for teaching me, guiding me, and showing me paths I hadn't yet seen. Your lessons have shaped who I am today.

Thank you to each of you for the role you've played in my life. I wouldn't be here without you, and I feel blessed to be in a world with you.

About The Author

Charell Star is a storyteller, foster care advocate, and firm believer in the power of purpose. A former foster youth herself, she's turned her journey into a mission to amplify unheard voices and spark change. She is honored to have served on the board of multiple foster-care related groups and has received numerous honors, including from the Court Appointed Special Advocates of New York City and the Congressional Coalition on Adoption Institute. In addition to her public speaking work, Charell's story has been featured in the series *Humans of New York* and the documentary *Feeling Wanted.*

When she's not writing or speaking, you can find her chasing down tennis balls, big laughs, and stories waiting to be told.

Connect with Charell on Instagram, TikTok, and Threads at @charellstar, visit her at www.charellstar.com or email her at contact@charellstar.com.

www.ingramcontent.com/pod-product-compliance
Lightning Source LLC
Chambersburg PA
CBHW061749120626
46550CB00005B/1936

* 9 7 9 8 9 9 1 9 2 2 8 0 7 *